hot, hot, hot!

PAUL GAYLER

cooking with fire and spice

photography by Gus Filgate

Kyle Cathie Limited

To my wife Anita and children – with love

This paperback edition published in 2004 by Kyle Cathie Limited,122 Arlington Road, London NW1 7HP

Originally published in Great Britain in 2000 as *Raising the Heat*

10 9 8 7 6 5 4 3 2 1

ISBN 1 85626 514 5

Text © 2000 Paul Gayler
Photography © 2000 Gus Filgate

Project editor Sheila Boniface   **Copy editor** Jane Middleton   **Home economist** Linda Tubby   **Stylist** Róisín Nield   **Designer** Vanessa Courtier   **Design Assistant** Gina Hochstein
Paul Gayler is hereby identified as the author of this work in accordance with Section 77 of the Copyright, Designs and Patents Act 1988

A CIP catalogue record for this title is available from the British Library
Printed and bound in Singapore by Tien Wah Press

contents

Introduction

I grew up in the East End of London at a time when fish and chips and jellied eels were the norm. My father ran a café for a while, which became a Chinese restaurant after he sold it. I took the opportunity of working there for a brief period while I was at college and the food made a lasting impression on me. It was my first encounter with spices and exotic flavourings. Chinese cooks use spices as much for their fragrance as for their heat, particularly star anise, ginger, garlic and sesame. Later, as a chef, I followed the usual classical French path but I also made a point of working in Indian restaurants, where I was amazed by the beguiling array of spices, with their jewel-like shades of ruby red, glowing orange and deep ochre. In Indian cooking as many as a dozen spices may be blended together to flavour one dish. On a working visit to Singapore and Malaysia, I learnt that chillies and other fiery ingredients were valuable not only for their heat but for their subtle, complex flavours. In Southeast Asia, the heat is tempered by cooling ingredients, such as coconut milk, lime juice and lemongrass, to produce an aromatic, perfectly balanced cuisine.

In 1990 I joined the Lanesborough and became acquainted with an entirely different style of spicing – that of the American Southwest, which borrows heavily from Mexican cooking. The Lanesborough is twinned with the Mansion on Turtle Creek in Dallas, one of the world's top hotels. Its head chef, Dean Fearing, is a leading exponent of Southwestern cuisine. Based on corn, beans, squashes, spices and chillies, with a plentiful supply of good meat and seafood, this is full of vigorous, sundrenched flavours. Hearty stews are fired up with spices and dried chillies (chile con carne is a Southwestern dish rather than a Mexican one), while simple roasts and grills are served with spicy relishes and barbecue sauces. What started as cowboy cooking is becoming increasingly refined under chefs like Dean, yet nothing prepared me for the subtleties of genuine Mexican cooking, which I experienced when Alicia De'Angeli of the El Tajin restaurant in Mexico City visited the Lanesborough with a team of chefs for a promotion on Mexican food. They taught me about the intricacies of using dried chillies and layering flavours. Mexican cuisine is not necessarily hot. The piquancy can easily be controlled, and chillies add interest and flavour, not just fire.

Besides oriental flavours, I have also learned to love the warm spices of North Africa and the Mediterranean (cumin, saffron, cinnamon, coriander, paprika) and the vibrant cooking of the Caribbean, which combines palate-singeing chillies with wonderful tropical fruits and vegetables. Over the years, my fascination with hot foods has remained undimmed. I would rather eat a curry or a Chinese meal than just about anything else, and I am not alone in this. Once people start to eat spicy food they tend to get hooked. The scientific explanation is that the sensation of pain when you consume chillies and other hot spices releases endorphins in the body, which cause a 'high'. This pain/pleasure equation means that some chilli addicts think the hotter the better. Personally, I believe there's more to spicy food than a blast of heat, stimulating though that can be. It is not until you explore the full range of chillies that you realise how complex the underlying flavours are, and that these, too, make a vital contribution. The pasilla, for example, a favourite chilli in Mexico and America's Southwest, has a rich, raisiny, almost chocolatey taste, while the mighty habanero has a fruity flavour and the heat of the jalapeño is offset by sweetness.

Although chillies reign supreme in the world of hot foods, they are not the only way of adding fire to your cooking. Other spicy ingredients include mustard, horseradish, ginger, peppercorns and some leaves, such as rocket, mizuna and the curry leaf. Even sausages, such as the Spanish chorizo and the North African merguez, have a role to play. Mustard, horseradish and pepper can rival chillies in heat, while ginger has a slow burn that refreshes and warms at the same time. Leaves tend to be only mildly spicy, useful for pepping up a salad or vegetable dish. Very often it is the combination of flavourings that provides a dish's heat – something oriental cooks understand well, with their unique spice blends such as the Chinese five-spice powder and the Indian garam masalas.

Raising the Heat is something of a whirlwind tour around the spicy cuisines of the world. You may find your head begins to spin as you turn from an incendiary South Indian curry to a sizzling-hot Szechuan-style stir-fry, then to a classic Italian pasta *arrabbiata* or Mexican *mole*. But the exhilarating thing about hot foods is that there are no restrictions – they can be enjoyed within the context of just about any nation's cooking (even we British have our horseradish sauce and hot mustards). Although I have included some classics, I don't claim that all these recipes are authentic (anyway it's virtually impossible to reproduce another country's dishes accurately – better to develop them to suit the produce available). In fact I am a bit of a culinary tart in this respect. As a hot-food addict, I have picked up ideas for spicy dishes on my travels around the world but I find it impossible to be faithful to any one type of cooking. I love combining a Cajun technique, say, with Asian spices to create a new fish dish, or a Mexican sauce with an Eastern-style treatment for meat or poultry. My cooking has always tended towards this sort of culinary promiscuity, but recently combining flavours and techniques from different cuisines has become fashionable and earned itself a label – fusion food.

Fusion food first took off in America and Australia, where you can find some of the most exciting and intelligent examples of the trend. All too often, though, fusion can lead to confusion – throwing ingredients together just for novelty's sake doesn't work. To put a new spin on old favourites, it's essential to learn the basics first and to understand how flavours work together. Then you can open your mind to new ideas. As far as spicy foods go, this means showing some restraint. Try to balance the flavours and textures of each dish, and don't choose an entire menu of chilli-hot dishes. Contrast is important. In hot countries, where most spicy food originates (because, curiously enough, hot food cools you down), this is often done by combining a hot dish with a cooling relish – think of the yogurt raita of India, the mint labna of the Middle East and the fruity salsas of Mexico.

You may notice that there are a lot of recipes for seafood in this book. This is partly because people are eating more fish now but also because I find it has a real affinity with spices – not just robust fish, such as tuna and mackerel, but more delicate ones like sole and cod. Seafood such as lobster and scallops is usually given a classical treatment but its firm, sweet flesh makes the perfect partner for chillies and other hot ingredients – try Goan red Masala Lobster (page 66), or Grilled scallops with black bean and citrus chilli oil vinaigrette (page 35), if you remain unconvinced.

If you are fairly new to spicy food, there are plenty of mild dishes in this book that you can make in order to acclimatise yourself before working up to the really hot stuff. Try the Celeriac and Mustard Soup (page 15), for example, or the Cioppino (page 64) to experience a gentle warming glow rather than blazing heat. If you are a real chilli aficionado, on the other hand, you may want to plunge straight into Fiery Keralan chicken (page 74) or Prawns piri-piri (page 65). Whatever your preference, you can control the heat level yourself by the amount of spicing you add. If in any doubt about the chilli tolerance of your guests, season your main dishes cautiously but serve them with fiery condiments or relishes (see Sauces and spices mixes on pages 142–157) so that they can spice their own food.

You won't need any special equipment for the recipes in this book but it is essential to have a powerful blender or food processor for making spice pastes and sauces. A spice grinder is also useful but a coffee mill or pestle and mortar will do instead. Although some of the ingredients may seem unfamiliar, it's surprising what you can buy at large supermarkets nowadays, while most big cities have Asian or Chinese food shops, which are an invaluable source of reasonably priced spices and fresh herbs. More and more shops supply by mail order now, or over the internet.

I hope the recipes in this book will set both your imagination and palate alight. Raise the heat in your cooking and explore the full range of fiery flavours from around the world.

All recipes serve 4 unless otherwise stated. ✳ indicates extra hot dishes.

The hot store cupboard – a guide to hot and spicy ingredients

Chillies – the ultimate heat

Chilli is the common name given to the fruit of a type of capsicum, grown all over the world but particularly in countries with a spicy cuisine, such as Mexico, India and the Caribbean. There are at least 200 varieties, varying from mild to searingly hot, and they come in a range of colours, shapes and sizes. They all share the same pod-like construction, however, with a central cavity containing small white seeds. The seeds and ribs contain most of the chilli's capsaicin, the volatile oil that is the source of its heat.

Fresh chillies are green until they ripen, when they turn red or, in some cases, yellow, orange, purple or black. Some varieties are sold both ripe and unripe. Ripe chillies can be just as fiery as green ones but they tend to have a sweeter, more distinct vegetable flavour. In general, the larger the chilli the milder it is, but this cannot be absolutely relied upon; even chillies from the same plant can vary greatly in strength. The best varieties are arguably produced in the West, although I'm sure the Asians would have something to say on that score. Certainly the most fragrant chillies come from South America. Once chillies are dried, their potency increases and their flavour becomes more complex, aided by a huge concentration of natural sugars. Their depth of flavour makes them an invaluable addition to sauces and slow-cooked braises and stews. As a rough rule of thumb, dried chillies can be divided into two categories – small hot ones and large mild ones – although, as with fresh chillies, there are lots of exceptions. Below is a guide to the chillies used in this book, with a rating out of ten to give an indication of their heat. Remember, though, that the only way of knowing for sure how hot an individual chilli is is to taste it. In Mexico, they bite into them before use.

Buying and Storing Chillies

Fresh With more and more varieties available from mail order and specialist shops finding the right chilli is not generally a problem. Even in supermarkets you may find individual types labelled by name. More often, however, there will just be one or two anonymous varieties –

these are probably Lombok or some form of Cayenne. Whatever sort of chilli you buy, make sure they are firm, shiny and unwrinkled, without any soft spots. They will keep in the fridge for up to 3 weeks if thoroughly wrapped in paper towel. Do not store them in plastic bags as the moisture created will cause them to shrivel. Left out in the air, they tend to wrinkle and lose flavour.

Dried When buying dried chillies, choose ones that are uniform in shape and avoid any that are faded or dusty. They should have a good aroma and, although dried, they should have some degree of flexibility, indicating freshness. Do not buy too many dried chillies at once; to enjoy them at their best they should be used within three months of purchase. Store in an airtight container to preserve their fragrant qualities.

Preparing Chillies

Chillies can literally burn, and should be handled with care. The capsaicin, which is concentrated in the ribs and seeds and present in smaller quantities in the flesh, is the culprit. If you have any cuts on your hands, or if you rub your eyes after preparing chillies, the pain can be excruciating. For protection, I suggest you wear thin rubber gloves, which can be thrown away afterwards. Thin-skinned chillies have the highest level of capsaicin.

Some recipes in this book call for chillies to be deseeded, while in others the seeds are left in. This is a way of controlling the heat; if the chillies are too hot for your taste, then remove the seeds – and cut off the ribs as well if you prefer. You will still be left with all the flavour, which is in the flesh. With dried chillies the capsaicin is spread throughout the chilli, so deseeding them doesn't make much difference to the degree of heat. When a recipe specifies chopped chillies, simply remove the stem end, cut the chilli in half down the centre and then use a small knife to scrape out the seeds, if you prefer. Cut the chilli into small dice with a sharp knife or scissors. Always wash your hands in hot soapy water before continuing with the recipe.

Large fresh chillies such as the poblano and New Mexican have tough skins, so it is common to roast and peel them before use (see below).

Roasting Fresh Chillies Roasting brings out the full flavour of fresh chillies and fills the air with a matchless fragrance. Simply place the chillies directly over a gas flame and leave for about 2–3 minutes, turning with tongs occasionally, until they are blistered and blackened all over. If you don't have a gas stove, grill about 5cm (2in) away from the heat, turning frequently, until charred. Or you can roast them in an oven preheated to 200°C/400°F/gas mark 6 for 5–6 minutes, drizzled with a little olive oil. When the chillies are ready, place them in a plastic bag, tie to seal it, and leave for 10–15 minutes; the steam created will help loosen the skins. Rinse the chillies under cold water, peel off the skins with a small knife and then use as required.

Roasting Dried Chillies In South American countries, dried chillies are usually roasted and then rehydrated in hot water before use. Remove the stem from the chillies and shake out the seeds, then place the chillies on a baking tray and roast for 2–3 minutes in an oven preheated to 190°C/375°F/gas mark 5. Alternatively, place under the grill on a low heat. Take great care not to burn or scorch the chillies, or they will taste bitter.

Putting Out the Fire

If your mouth is left burning after eating hot chillies, don't drink water or beer, which will only spread the capsaicin further and make things worse. Instead, try dairy products, such as milk, cheese, yoghurt or ice cream, which will help neutralise the heat. I know people who swear by eating bread, or even a spoonful of sugar.

Fresh Chillies

Bird's Eye (8/10) These tiny, explosive chilies are used in Thai cooking and can be green, orange or red. They are very similar to Thai chillies (see below).

Habanero (10/10) Sometimes confused with the Scotch bonnet, this is probably the hottest chilli available, said to be 75 times hotter than the jalapeño, so beware! The habanero is lantern shaped, measuring about 5cm (2in) long and 4cm (1½in) wide, and comes in all colours, although yellow and red are the most common. Despite its intense heat, the habanero has a fruity tone that goes particularly well with dishes containing tropical fruits and tomatoes. It is generally deseeded and used very sparingly in salsas, sauces, stews and marinades. So fierce is this chilli that it can irritate the skin, so take great care when handling.

Hungarian Cherry Chilli Pepper (3/10) This round, thick, fleshy chilli contains a lot of seeds. It is quite sweet when ripe, with a medium heat. Use in soups or salads, or stuff with a meat or cheese filling and bake.

Hungarian Hot Wax (4/10) This large, long, slightly twisted chilli starts yellow and matures to an orange-red colour. It can grow up to 13cm (5in) in length and is generally used for frying, in spicy salads or for dressings.

Jalapeño (5/10) A shiny, torpedo-shaped, bright-green chilli from the state of Veracruz in Mexico. Measuring 5–7.5cm (2–3in) in length, it was originally very hot, although it now seems to vary and can be fairly mild. It is the most common chilli in the United States and is great for making spicy salsas, dips and pizza toppings, or as a flavouring for cornbread (see page 136). The jalapeño is also sold ripe and red, when it is slightly sweeter and less hot.

Lombok (3/10) These long, thin chillies originate from Indonesia but are now the commonest variety found in big stores and supermarkets sometimes simply labelled mild chillies. Use in soups, salsas and stir-fries.

New Mexican (5/10) This moderately hot, elongated chilli is sometimes known as the long green chilli. It is used in sauces, stews and salsas and, like the poblano, can be stuffed to make the classic Mexican dish, *chiles rellenos*. It is wonderful roasted, which brings out its sweet, rather fruity flavour.

Poblano (3/10) This impressive-looking chilli has a purple-black tinge to its dark green flesh and resembles a green pepper in appearance and in size, but tapers down from the shoulders to a point. It is usually mild. Poblanos are always roasted and peeled before use, as they have a tough skin that is not easily digestible. Roasting gives them a smoky, even earthy flavour. They are used in sauces, especially Mexican *mole* sauces, or stuffed to make *chiles rellenos*, then dipped in batter and deep-fried. When dried, the poblano is known as the ancho chilli (see below).

Serrano (7/10) This small chilli has a lively heat and is available both unripened (green) and ripe (red), although red is more common. It is generally used in salsas and in the classic Mexican guacamole. You can also roast it and use in sauces to give them a little more bite. It is also available pickled.

Thai (8/10) Also known as the Japanese or Asian chilli, this is small and narrow and can be red or green in colour. It has meaty flesh, with a high proportion of seeds and an intriguing, lingering heat. Use sparingly unless you have a high chilli tolerance. Thai chillies are good added whole to Thai-style curries and stir-fries. If they are not available, substitute two serrano chillies for each Thai chilli. They are at their freshest when sold in small clusters.

Dried Chillies

Ancho (4/10) The ancho is a dried poblano chilli that has become wrinkled and deep red. It measures 10–13cm (4–5in) in length and 7.5cm (3in) wide across the top (*ancho* means wide in Spanish). It is the fruitiest and sweetest of the dried chillies, rich yet mild in flavour, and is generally soaked and puréed to make Mexican-style sauces and *moles*.

Cascabel (4/10) The cascabel derives its name from the Spanish for rattle, the sound given off by the seeds when these little round chillies are shaken. They have a smoky, slightly acidic flavour. Sauces, stews and salsas all benefit from their nutty, assertive taste.

Chipotle (7/10) This is a dried smoked jalapeño, with a deep, well-rounded heat and a smoky-sweet chocolatey flavour. It is generally used in sauces, soups and salsas but is good in almost anything. Chipotles are also available canned in red adobo sauce.

De Arbol (8/10) This long, red-black, pointed chilli is fiery yet grassy in flavour, with a searing heat. Use in sauces and soups and for making chilli oil. It is widely available in powdered form and is also available fresh, when it is small and green.

Guajillo (4/10) A long, tender, thin-fleshed chilli with a deep orange colour. It is moderately hot and has a slightly tangy, fruity taste with a green tea overtone. The guajillo is often combined with other varieties to give dishes a distinct flavour and orange tint.

New Mexican Red (4/10) A bright-scarlet, thin-fleshed chilli with a sweet, cherry-like flavour, this has a smooth, crisp and clean heat. It is indispensable for making red chilli sauce and is also sold powdered or in flakes. It is thought by many to be the doyenne of chillies – quite a reputation to live up to!

Pasilla (4/10) Sometimes known as the chile negro (black chilli), this tastes like dried raisins but with a slightly herby overtone. It has a medium heat and is great in Mexican mole sauces, with seafood or sautéed with woodland mushrooms.

Peperoncino (6/10) An orange-red Italian chilli with a hot, sweet flavour. It is commonly used in tomato-based dishes and is also good with seafood.

Chilli Powders

Cayenne Pepper Originally from the Cayenne region of French Guyana, this is ground from the dried, small, hot chilli of the same name. It is very pungent, with a sharp bite, so use sparingly.

Chilli Powder This is the most readily obtainable form of chilli. However, I find it gives heat but no real flavour, as it is usually blended with other ingredients such as herbs and spices which detract from the taste. Use only in an emergency. Alternatively, you can make your own very easily by roasting dried chillies (see page 8), then grinding them in a spice mill or coffee grinder. Store in jars or airtight bags. The advantage of making chilli powder yourself is that you can use whatever type of chilli you prefer, or a combination. My favourite for this purpose is the New Mexican Red.

Dried Chilli Flakes These are simply crushed dried chillies, including the seeds. They are useful for pepping up all manner of dishes, including pasta sauces and pizzas. Dried red chilli flakes are the most common but you might also be able to find crushed green jalapeño flakes, which have a sweet yet fiery flavour.

Paprika Paprika is ground from a dried sweet red pepper, the *Capsicum annum*. There are two types: hot paprika, from Hungary, which is almost as fierce as cayenne, and mild (sweet) paprika from Spain, which has a wonderful smoky flavour. Both are used in soups, stews (such as the Hungarian *gulyás*, or goulash) and sausages.

Chilli Sauces, Pastes and Condiments

Chilli Jelly Popular in Southwest American cooking, this spicy-sweet jelly (see page 148) is wonderful for glazing meat or can be served as a relish – it is particularly good with duck.

Chilli Oil Widely used in oriental cooking, this is made by steeping hot chillies in a bland oil such as groundnut. It is used as a condiment, in dressings, or added to dishes after cooking. You will find a recipe for chilli oil and some interesting variations on page 152.

Harissa Reasonable versions of this North African chilli paste can be bought in tubes or tins. To experience it at its best, though, it's worth making your own (see page 156).

Hot Pepper Sauce A thin, red, West Indian sauce made from habanero chillies, with enough bite to flavour anything. Use sparingly in sauces and salsas.

Mexican Chilli Sauce This is a fiery, thin red sauce, used to flavour meat for enchiladas and other Mexican dishes. The commercial product tends to be a poor substitute for the real thing (see recipe on page 146), although it is useful to have in stock for emergencies.

Mexican Salsas Mexican salsas are simple chunky relishes made from finely chopped fresh ingredients such as tomatoes, onions or even fruit, spiked with chilli and herbs. This is one area where there really is no substitute for making your own. Most salsas are very simple to prepare, with little or no cooking involved – it's just a question of chopping your ingredients and leaving them to marinate for a short while. (Try the recipes on pages 150–151).

Sambal In Southeast Asia, especially Indonesia, there is a whole family of sambals – pungent pastes served in small quantities for dipping. They are available from most Asian stores, or try the recipe on page 148.

Spicy Bean Sauce A dark, pungent Chinese seasoning paste made from black beans, garlic, ginger, soy sauce and lots of chilli. Look for a good-quality commercial product and use it to enliven sauces and stir-fries, especially if you like your food hot. Or mix with sweet chilli sauce to make a condiment.

Sweet Chilli Sauce Used in Asian cookery, this is just as it sounds – a spicy yet sweet-tasting sauce, great for stir-fries, sauces and dressings. It's easy to buy but almost as easy to make – try the recipe on page 147.

Tabasco Sauce A ferociously hot, thin, almost citric liquid, made in Louisiana from puréed cayenne chillies and vinegar. It gives a wonderful kick to soups and sauces. I am a member of the Tabasco Club, an informal association of Tabasco lovers, which was formed in appreciation of this addictive ingredient.

Spice mixes

Cajun Spice Mix Used in Creole and Cajun cooking in America's Deep South, this is a punchy blend of chilli, spices, dried herbs and garlic (see the recipe on page 157). It is generally rubbed over fish or meat before grilling or roasting .

Chinese Five-spice Powder A fragrant blend of cinnamon, star anise, Szechuan pepper, cloves and fennel seeds, this is now available in most supermarkets. Use for spicing up meat and fish. It is particularly good for marinades and slow-cooked dishes.

Curry Powders and Pastes Curry is not an Indian word at all, but a term the British Colonials applied to all Indian spice blends. Jars of curry powder or paste can be bought ready-made but in India no such spice mix is recognised, as cooks always prepare their own fragrant blends. These vary from region to region and according to personal taste and what dish it is being used for. Bought curry powder or paste is a convenient stand-by but once opened it quickly becomes stale. It doesn't take very long to make your own and it will pay dividends in terms of flavour. I have included several of my favourite curry powders and spice mixes in this book (see pages 156–157).

Garam Masala Garam masala means 'hot spices' and is a mixture of cinnamon, cardamom, cloves, cumin, black pepper and other spices according to taste. It is generally added to dishes at the last moment to enliven the flavours. Commercial versions rapidly deteriorate in flavour, so it is a good idea to mix up your own – preferably using freshly ground spices (page 66).

Indian Five-Spice Powder This aromatic spice mix is not as well known as the Chinese five-spice powder.

It consists of equal measures of ground cumin, black mustard, fenugreek, fennel and nigella seeds. It is not always sold as a mix, so if you cannot find it, buy the seeds whole and grind them yourself – even better!

Other hot spices

Galangal

Widely used in Southeast Asian cooking, this rhizome is related to ginger and has a similar flavour, although more citrussy. There are two varieties, greater and lesser galangal, and it is the lesser that has the stronger flavour. Use in the same way as ginger, which can be substituted if galangal is unavailable.

Ginger

This knobbly, aromatic rhizome is an essential ingredient in Asian cooking and is popular the world over. It has a light brown skin, which is always peeled off before use, and juicy, pale yellow flesh, with a sharp refreshing flavour. Store, tightly wrapped, in the refrigerator, where it will keep for several weeks.

Pickled Pink Ginger A staple of Japanese cooking, this ingredient is made by preserving paper-thin slices of young ginger root in a vinegar solution. It is traditionally used as a seasoning or condiment for sushi and sashimi.

Mustard

Mustard is the name given to the seeds of the yellow, black or brown mustard plant, the black being the hottest. Mixed with wine or vinegar and seasonings, it is a favourite spice the world over, although styles vary according to country. The Chinese, for example, prefer hot mustard, the Scandinavians sweet mustard. The texture can be smooth or coarse, and flavourings such as tarragon or honey are often added.

Dijon Mustard This is a smooth, pale-yellow, clean-tasting mustard made from black or brown seeds blended with verjuice (unripe grape juice), salt and spices. It is usually quite mild, although it can vary in strength. Dijon mustard is used in classic French-style sauces and salad dressings.

English Mustard English mustard is sharp and slightly acidic in flavour, and is available as a powder or made into a paste. Traditionally it is served as an accompaniment to roast beef and other meats.

Grain Mustard To make grain mustard the seeds are partly crushed and partly ground, to give a crunchy texture, then mixed with spices, vinegar and sometimes other flavourings, too. It is usually medium hot and is good served with cold meats and sausages. Meaux mustard is a favourite of mine and I am also very fond of the green peppercorn variety.

Mustard Oil This is used in India in the same way as ghee, and is available from Indian and Asian grocers. It is golden brown and extremely pungent, and may be sold pure or blended with other oils. Mustard oil is also used in commercial salad dressings and in the Italian *mostarda di Cremona*, or *mostarda di frutta* (mixed candied fruits in mustard syrup).

Mustard Seeds Black mustard seeds are widely used in Indian cooking, both whole and ground. The whole seeds are usually dry-roasted first to extract the fragrance. Most mustard is made from brown mustard seeds, while yellow seeds are used for mild American mustards and for pickling.

Pepper

Sometimes known as the king of spices, the peppercorn is the fruit of the vine pepper, *Piper nigrum*. Each variety has a different aroma and taste, all with the underlying heat of basic black pepper.

Black Peppercorns The familiar black peppercorn is picked while green and then left to dry, when it wrinkles and blackens. It is very pungent and fiery.

Green Peppercorns These are unripe fresh peppercorns, preserved by bottling in brine or vinegar or, more recently, by freeze-drying. It is milder in flavour than black pepper, with a clean, fresh taste.

Mignonette Pepper Widely used in France, this is a rough mixture of cracked black and white peppercorns.

Pink Peppercorns This is not a peppercorn at all but an aromatic berry native to South America. Available dried or bottled in vinegar, it has a brittle, slightly bitter skin. I find the bottled variety has a better flavour.

Sansho Also called Japanese pepper, this is the ground dried leaves of the tree that produces Szechuan pepper but its character is entirely different. It has a citrus fragrance with a hint of lychee and a mild, peppery taste. Look for it in Japanese shops.

Szechuan Pepper Like pink pepper, this is not a member of the peppercorn family but a dried berry. It comes from a small tree, native to China, and has a spicy, peppery flavour. It is used throughout Asia but particularly in Chinese cooking. Szechuan peppercorns are normally roasted before use to bring out their wonderful flavour. You should be able to find them in Chinese shops or large supermarkets. If necessary, freshly ground black pepper can be substituted.

White Peppercorns These are picked when ripe, then soaked in water to remove the outer coating and dried. They are hotter and less fragrant than black pepper.

Wasabi

Also known as Japanese horseradish, wasabi is a fierce, heady condiment available in powder or paste form. When mixed with water, it is much stronger than fresh horseradish. It is widely used in Japanese cooking, particularly in sushi.

Spicy ingedients

Horseradish

Horseradish is a large, knarled white root. Fresh horseradish, usually available in early spring, must be peeled and grated before use but it gives off such powerful vapours that this task can bring tears to the eyes. However, it's worth persevering, as the flavour is incomparable. It is also available ready grated in jars, which makes a reasonable substitute, or dried and powdered. Try to avoid ready-made horseradish sauces, which are generally full of unnecessary additives.

Leaves

Curry Leaves These are not related to curry powder. Used in South Indian cooking, they are the small, almond-shaped leaves of the curry plant and have a warm, spicy flavour. Asian shops sell dried curry leaves and occasionally fresh ones, which are much better. If you can find only dried curry leaves you will need to use at least twice as many, since the flavour is weaker. Fresh leaves will keep in the fridge for a week or so.

Mustard Leaves The mustard plant is a prized vegetable throughout India and is fast becoming a fashionable salad leaf in the West. Of the several varieties available I think mizuna is the best. It has green leaves with a ragged edge and a slightly spicy flavour.

Nasturtium Leaves Nasturtiums grow in many people's gardens but few realise that they make a delightful addition to soups and salads, too. They have a pungent flavour and aroma, reminiscent of caper berries, and should be used with discretion. The leaves (and flowers, which have a peppery taste) make an interesting addition to sandwiches and are also good with cheese dishes.

Rocket Rocket tends to be considered as a salad leaf but in Italy this peppery plant has always been used in cooking, too, particularly in pasta sauces and soups. It also makes a fine pesto. Wild rocket has a more assertive taste than the cultivated variety.

Watercress An aquatic member of the mustard family, this has a vigorous, peppery flavour. Too often relegated to the role of garnish, it makes excellent purées, sauces and soups.

Radishes

Radishes were first cultivated in China, Japan and India but they are now found in all temperate regions of Europe. There are a great many varieties – round, long, pink, black, white, green and purple. They are normally eaten raw but the leaves of pink radishes can also be cooked like spinach.

Sausages

Using spicy sausages in cooking is an easy way of adding fire to your food. Here are some of my favourites:

Andouille Not to be confused with the milder French sausage of the same name, this spicy, heavily smoked pork sausage is a speciality of Louisiana. It is an essential ingredient in jambalaya, gumbo and other Cajun dishes.

Chorizo This Spanish pork sausage contains paprika, which gives it both its heat and its colour. Available both smoked and unsmoked, it is used in both Spanish and Mexican cooking.

Kielbasa This is a spicy boiling sausage from Poland, made of beef and pork, garlic and black pepper.

Merguez Full of North African spicing, this lamb sausage can be searingly hot. It originates from Algeria but is now used throughout North Africa and is popular in France, too.

Peperone A coarse sausage from Italy, flavoured with fennel, spices and chilli.

soups and starters

Thai-inspired pumpkin and basil soup

If you can find Thai basil, which is sometimes available from Asian grocer's shops, the soup will have a more authentic flavour. But it's delicious made with ordinary basil, too.

Heat the butter in a frying pan, add the diced pumpkin and fry for 3–4 minutes, until coloured. Add the onion, garlic, galangal or ginger and chilli and cook for 2 minutes. Stir in the paste and cook for 1 minute, until fragrant. Add the chicken stock and bring to the boil, then reduce the heat and simmer until the pumpkin is just tender. Finally, stir in the coconut milk and torn basil leaves and season to taste.

Serve immediately in 4 individual bowls.

25g (1oz) unsalted butter

450g (1lb) pumpkin or butternut squash, peeled and cut into 1cm (1/2in) dice

1 onion, chopped

2 garlic cloves, crushed

1 teaspoon finely chopped fresh galangal or ginger

1 Thai chilli, thinly sliced

1 tablespoon Red Thai Curry Paste (see p155)

1 litre (13/4 pints) chicken stock

175ml (6fl oz) coconut milk

8 basil leaves, torn into small pieces

Salt and freshly ground black pepper

Celeriac and mustard soup

Back in 1979 I was asked to prepare an eight-course vegetarian dinner for 250 people for a diamond company in Antwerp, Belgium. The meal was a great success and I brought the recipe for this soup back from Antwerp. It is beautifully creamy with just a little mustard bite.

Melt the butter in a large saucepan, add the leek, then cover and cook over a low heat for about 5 minutes, until soft. Add the diced celeriac, and potatoes and sweat for 5 minutes. Stir in 1 table-spoon of the mustard and the chicken stock, bring to the boil, then reduce the heat and simmer until the vegetables are tender. Place in a blender and blitz until smooth.

Return the soup to a clean saucepan, stir in the double cream and the remaining mustard and reheat gently. Sprinkle with the chopped chives before serving.

25g (1oz) unsalted butter

1 small leek, chopped

1 medium-sized celeriac, peeled and chopped

2 potatoes, peeled and chopped

2 tablespoons Dijon mustard

1 litre well-flavoured chicken stock

150ml (1/4 pint) double cream

1 tablespoon chopped chives

Black bean and squid ink soup

If you prefer, you could blitz this soup to a smooth purée rather than leaving it rough-textured. Either way, it's a wonderful warming bowlful.

Place the soaked beans in a large pot, cover with water and bring to the boil. Drain the beans in a colander and then return to the pan. Add the chicken stock or water and bring to the boil, then add the garlic and thyme and reduce the heat to a simmer. Cook for 1–11/2 hours, then stir in the vegetables and jalapeño chillies and simmer for 30 minutes, until everything is tender.

Place the mixture in a blender and blitz to a coarse texture. Return to a clean pan and bring back to the boil. Season to taste, stir in the squid ink and lemon juice and keep warm.

Gently heat the chilli oil in a frying pan, season the squid with salt and pepper and fry quickly for 1 minute. Serve in individual bowls, topped with the sautéed squid and sprinkled with the coriander.

HOT TIP Squid ink is available in small sachets from some fishmongers.

Serves 4–6

150g (5oz) black beans, soaked overnight and then drained

1.2 litres (2 pints) chicken stock or water

1 garlic clove, chopped

1 teaspoon fresh thyme

1 carrot, finely diced

1 onion, finely diced

2 celery sticks, finely diced

1 red pepper, roasted, peeled and finely diced

2 green jalapeño chillies, deseeded and finely diced

2 tablespoons squid ink

Juice of 1/2 lemon

4 tablespoons Chilli Oil (see page 152)

150g (5oz) baby squid, cleaned and cut into rings

2 tablespoons chopped coriander

Salt and freshly ground black pepper

Chilled smoky tomato soup
with paprika soured cream

Preheat the grill to its highest setting. Put the tomatoes in a bowl and toss them with half the olive oil, then place on the grill rack. Place under the hot grill for 8–10 minutes or until they are soft and slightly charred.

Heat the remaining oil in a large pan, add the onion, garlic, cumin, coriander and half the paprika and fry gently until softened but not coloured. Add the cherry chilli peppers, followed by the charred tomatoes and the tomato purée and cook over a low heat for 5 minutes. Pour on the chicken stock and bring to the boil, then reduce the heat and simmer for 2 minutes. Pass the soup through a fine sieve. Add the vinegar and sugar, return the soup to the boil and simmer for 3–5 minutes. Remove from the heat, leave to cool and then chill. Season with salt and pepper when cold.

To serve, ladle into individual soup bowls. Blend together the soured cream and the remaining paprika, top each bowlful with a dollop of cream and sprinkle over a little extra paprika. Stir in gently to create a decorative swirl.

HOT TIP Don't purée this soup in a blender – it tends to lose its colour and becomes a washed-out shade of pink.

1.5kg (3½lb) ripe but firm plum tomatoes, halved

4 tablespoons olive oil

1 onion, chopped

2 garlic cloves, crushed

2 teaspoons ground cumin

1/2 teaspoon ground coriander

2 teaspoons smoked paprika, plus extra to garnish

2 Hungarian cherry chilli peppers, deseeded and chopped

1 tablespoon tomato purée

900ml (1½ pints) chicken stock

4 tablespoons balsamic vinegar

1½ tablespoons caster sugar

4 tablespoons soured cream

Salt and freshly ground black pepper

Romaine lettuce and nasturtium soup

Nasturtium leaves add a delicate, peppery flavour to this simple summer soup, which can also be served chilled. If you can't find any nasturtiums, they are very easy to grow, with the added bonus that the flowers can be used to garnish salads.

Wash and shred the lettuce and nasturtium leaves. Melt the butter in a pan, add the onion and leek and sweat for 4–5 minutes, until softened. Add the shredded lettuce and nasturtium leaves, then pour over the stock, season with a little salt and bring to the boil. Add the potatoes, reduce the heat and simmer until the potatoes are tender.

Place in a blender and blitz to a smooth purée. Return to the pan, add the cream and simmer for 2–3 minutes. Add a pinch of sugar and season.

Pour into individual serving bowls and garnish with shredded nasturtium leaves.

400g (14oz) romaine (Cos) lettuce

25g (1oz) fresh nasturtium leaves, plus extra to garnish

25g (1oz) unsalted butter

1 onion, roughly chopped

1 leek, chopped

750ml (1¼ pints) well-flavoured chicken stock

150g (5oz) potatoes, peeled and chopped

150ml (1/4 pint) single cream or milk

A pinch of sugar

Salt and freshly ground black pepper

CHILLED SMOKY TOMATO SOUP

Arepa soup
(creamed green chilli polenta soup with shellfish)

This is an adaptation of a soup I had in one of America's best-loved Mexican restaurants.

Scrub the mussels and clams under cold running water, de-bearding the mussels and discarding any open ones that don't close when tapped on a work surface. Place the mussels and clams in a large pan with the shallots and half the chilli, pour over the white wine and chicken stock, then cover the pan and cook over a high heat for 3–4 minutes, shaking the pan occasionally, until the shells open. Drain the mussels and clams in a colander, then strain the cooking liquor into a clean pan. Bring to the boil, and add the milk. Rain in the polenta and

cook over a low heat, stirring constantly, for 4–5 minutes or until thickened.

Remove the mussels and clams from their shells. Place the polenta soup in a blender, add half the mussels and clams and half the sweetcorn and blitz to a smooth purée.

Return to the pan, add the cream and bring to the boil. Season to taste, then add the remaining mussels, clams and sweetcorn, together with the prawns.

Serve garnished with the remaining chilli.

1kg (2 1/4 lb) mussels
500g (18oz) clams
2 shallots, finely sliced
2 green chillies, finely sliced
100ml (3 1/2 fl oz) dry white wine
1 litre (1 3/4 pints) chicken stock
150ml (1/4 pint) full-fat milk
100g (4oz) polenta
200g (7oz) cooked sweetcorn
100ml (3 1/2 fl oz) double cream
100g (4oz) small Norwegian prawns
Salt and freshly ground black pepper

Caldo de albóndigas

This is a classic Mexican soup of spicy meatballs cooked in chicken broth. I find a lot of chicken broths tastless, with no depth or body. Here is an exception to the rule – a broth that is bursting with flavour. It is traditionally served with Spanish-style meatballs and accompanied by a smoky guacamole.

First prepare the meatballs by mixing all the ingredients together in a bowl. Season with salt and pepper, then, using your hands, shape the mixture into 20 small meatballs.

With a knife, remove the corn kernels from the cob. Bring the chicken stock to the boil in a large saucepan, add the corn and simmer for 10–12 minutes, then add the roasted chipotle chilli, mushrooms, garlic, cumin, coriander and tomatoes. Simmer for 5 minutes to allow the flavours to infuse. Carefully drop the meatballs into the broth and cook gently for 8–10 minutes. Add the thinly sliced red chilli and season with salt and freshly ground black pepper.

Put the meatballs into deep serving bowls and ladle the smoky-flavoured broth over them. Serve the tortilla strips and guacamole separately so your guests can help themselves.

1 corn on the cob

500ml (18fl oz) well-flavoured chicken stock (preferably home-made)

1 chipotle chilli, roasted (see p8)

150g (5oz) button mushrooms, sliced

1/2 garlic clove, crushed

1/2 teaspoon ground cumin

A handful of fresh coriander, stalks removed

2 plum tomatoes, skinned, deseeded and cut into 5mm (1/4in) dice

1 red jalapeño chilli, thinly sliced into rings

Salt and freshly ground black pepper

For the albóndigas (meatballs):

1/2 onion, grated

225g (8oz) minced pork

1 garlic clove, crushed

1 teaspoon cumin seeds

1/2 teaspoon dried red chilli flakes

1 egg, beaten

5 tablespoons fresh white breadcrumbs

1 tablespoon chopped coriander

To serve:

Fried tortilla strips

4 tablespoons Guacamole en Molcajete (see p153)

Chickpea and lentil mulligatawny
with smoked chicken and cumin yoghurt

Mulligatawny is one of those curious Anglo-Indian dishes that arose from the British occupation of India. The Victorians made it with onions, chicken, curry powder, desiccated coconut, and apple for sweetness. My version is much livelier, with chilli, turmeric, and a smoked chicken and cumin garnish.

Melt the butter in a pan, add the onion, garlic, chilli flakes and turmeric and cook over a low heat until softened. Add the soaked chickpeas and curry paste and cook for 5 minutes, then sprinkle over the gram flour and stir it in. Pour on the stock and bring to the boil, then simmer for 2 hours topping up with more liquid if it begins to get too dry. Stir in the lentils and simmer for 30–40 minutes, then add the mango chutney and apple and cook for another 20 minutes.

For the cumin yoghurt, toast the cumin seeds in a frying pan over a low heat until they are slightly darker and release their fragrance. Transfer to a spice mill or pestle and mortar and grind to a powder. Stir the cumin into the yoghurt and set aside.

Pour the soup into a blender and blitz to a smooth purée. Return to a clean pan, add the coconut milk and bring to the boil. Season to taste and serve, topped with the shredded smoked chicken and a little cumin yoghurt.

25g (1oz) unsalted butter

1 onion, finely chopped

1 garlic clove, crushed

1 teaspoon dried red chilli flakes

1/4 teaspoon ground turmeric

125g (41/2oz) chickpeas, soaked in water overnight and then drained

2 tablespoons My Curry Paste (see p154)

1 tablespoon gram (chickpea) flour

1 litre (13/4 pints) chicken or vegetable stock

125g (41/2oz) Puy lentils

1 tablespoon mango chutney

1 Granny Smith apple, peeled, cored and chopped

400ml/14oz can of coconut milk

2 cooked smoked chicken breasts, skin removed and meat shredded

Salt and freshly ground black pepper

For the cumin yoghurt:

1/2 teaspoon cumin seeds

6 tablespoons Greek yoghurt

Spicy channa
(roasted chickpeas)

A wonderful and simple snack of spice-roasted chickpeas. It is normally sold by street vendors in India but it is easy to prepare at home and makes a great accompaniment to drinks.

Preheat the oven to 180ºC/350ºF/gas mark 4. Toss the chickpeas with all the remaining ingredients, spread out on a baking sheet and place in the oven to toast for about 8–10 minutes, until golden brown and crunchy. Store in an airtight container if not used immediately.

250g (9oz) cooked chickpeas, well drained and dried

1/2 teaspoon cayenne pepper

25g (1oz) unsalted butter, melted

1/2 teaspoon My Curry Paste (see p154)

A pinch of brown sugar

Salt

Minced rabbit satay
with peanut and ginger dip

Marinating meat or fish and then grilling it on a skewer has been common for centuries, and is still popular today for barbecues. This Southeast Asian classic takes on a new twist when made with minced rabbit, but you could use chicken or pork instead. A fresh cucumber salad makes a good accompaniment.

For the satay, put all the ingredients except the rabbit and lemongrass in a blender or food processor and blitz to a wet paste. Place the minced rabbit in a bowl, pour over the paste and mix well with a wooden spoon. Cover and chill for 2 hours.

Meanwhile, make the dip: place all the ingredients in a pan and bring to the boil, then reduce the heat and simmer for 2–3 minutes. Pour into a bowl and leave to cool.

Remove the rabbit mixture from the refrigerator.

Dip your hands in a little hot water and then mould a heaped tablespoonful of the mixture around each prepared lemongrass skewer, making sure it encompasses it completely. Place the skewers under a hot grill or, better still, over a hot barbecue and grill until golden, turning occasionally. They should take about 5–6 minutes to cook.

Serve the charred satay skewers with the peanut and ginger dip, or with Chilli and Raisin Jam (see page 148) – or even with both.

1/2 teaspoon cumin seeds

1/2 teaspoon ground turmeric

1 garlic clove, chopped

2cm (3/4in) piece of fresh root ginger, chopped

1 large shallot, chopped

11/2 teaspoons demerara sugar

5 tablespoons groundnut or vegetable oil

1 tablespoon sesame oil

2 teaspoons nam pla (Thai fish sauce)

450g (1lb) minced rabbit (taken from the saddle or hind legs)

8 lemongrass stalks, outer layers removed, cut into 15cm (6in) lengths

Salt and freshly ground black pepper

For the peanut and ginger dip:

300ml (1/2 pint) well-flavoured chicken stock

2 teaspoons My Curry Paste (see p154)

1 garlic clove, crushed

1 jalapeño chilli, deseeded and finely chopped

1/2 teaspoon honey

1cm (1/2in) piece of fresh root ginger, finely chopped

6 tablespoons smooth peanut butter

1/2 teaspoon light soy sauce

A dash of wine vinegar

Crispy fried quail
with cashew and mint mole

This is a bit of a fusion dish, combining oriental and Mexican techniques. The quail are prepared in a similar way to Peking duck – brushed with a rich glaze and then dried – but they are served with a spicy, minty Mexican mole. *Mole* means sauce or concoction. It is usually made with chillies and the colour varies depending on what chillies are used.

Heat the maple syrup, chilli and lemon juice and brush all over the quail. Place in a dry, well-ventilated area for 8–12 hours, then brush with the glaze again.

For the mole, pour boiling water over the ancho chilli and leave to soak for 1 hour, then drain. Place the chillies, onion, garlic, red peppers, tomatoes and bread in a food processor and blitz to a paste, then add the cashews, spices and mint and process again.

Heat the oil in a frying pan, then pour in the mole mixture and fry for 8–10 minutes. Add a little water to bring it to the consistency of a puréed soup, then season with the sugar and some salt and pepper. Keep warm.

Heat some vegetable oil in a deep-fat fryer or a large, deep saucepan to 170°C/325°F. Deep-fry the quails for 8–10 minutes, until tender and crisp, then drain on kitchen paper.

Pour the sauce on to serving plates and top with the fried quail. I like to serve this with black beans and guacamole.

4 tablespoons maple syrup
1 New Mexican dried red chilli or
* 1/2 teaspoon chilli powder*
Juice of 1 lemon
8 quails, boned and cut in half
Vegetable oil for deep-frying
For the cashew and mint mole:
2 dried ancho chillies, roasted (see p8)
1 onion, roughly chopped
2 garlic cloves, crushed
1 red pepper, trimmed and deseeded
200g (7oz) can of plum tomatoes
3 slices of white bread, crusts removed
75g (3oz) cashew nuts
1/2 teaspoon ground cinnamon
1/2 teaspoon ground allspice
1 bunch of mint (about 50g/2oz)
4 tablespoons vegetable oil
A pinch of sugar
Salt and freshly ground black pepper

Potato and prawn bhajias
on saffron, cucumber and tomato raita

Make the raita by mixing all the ingredients together, then set aside.

Shred the potatoes – preferably on a mandoline, although you could do them on the coarse side of a grater. In a bowl, mix together all the dry ingredients for the batter, add the curry paste and then gradually add the water, stirring until combined. Season with salt. Add the potatoes, chillies and coriander and toss well together.

Heat some vegetable oil in a deep-fat fryer or a large, deep pan to 180°C/350°F. Season the prawns with salt and ground black pepper. Using a large tablespoon, scoop a mound of the batter mixture into the palm of your hand, then press a prawn into the centre and re-shape into a ball, so the prawn is in the middle. Repeat to make 16 bhajias. Fry them in batches in the hot oil for 3–4 minutes, until crisp and cooked through, then drain on kitchen paper.

Place the bhajias on a bed of the raita, on individual serving plates, garnish with fresh coriander leaves and serve immediately,

350g (12oz) potatoes, peeled

2 green Thai chillies, deseeded and chopped

50g (2oz) fresh coriander, chopped, plus some coriander leaves to garnish

Vegetable oil for deep-frying

16 raw tiger prawns, peeled and de-veined

Salt and freshly ground black pepper

For the raita:

1/2 cucumber, peeled, deseeded and cut into 1cm (1/2in) dice

6 tablespoons Greek yoghurt

1/4 teaspoon saffron strands, steeped in 2 tablespoons boiling water

1 teaspoon ground cumin

1 teaspoon ground coriander

1 tablespoon chopped mint

4 plum tomatoes, skinned, deseeded and cut into 1cm (1/2in) dice

For the batter:

100g (4oz) gram (chickpea) flour

50g (2oz) ground rice

1/2 teaspoon baking powder

1/2 teaspoon chilli powder

1/2 teaspoon ground turmeric

1/4 teaspoon asafoetida

1 tablespoon My Curry Paste (see p154)

225ml (7 1/2fl oz) water

Hot Chinese mustard chicken wings

Using a sharp knife, cut off the tip of each chicken wing. At this stage you can either leave the wings as they are or cut through the joint to make two smaller pieces.

In a large bowl, combine all the remaining ingredients, then add the chicken wings and mix thoroughly so they are well coated. Cover and leave to marinate for up to 12 hours.

Preheat the oven to 200°C/400°F/gas mark 6.

Remove the chicken wings from their marinade and place in a baking dish or tin, then roast in the oven for about 30 minutes. Pour the marinade into a small pan and bring to the boil. Simmer until reduced and thickened enough to coat the back of a spoon. Use this reduced marinade to baste the wings as they cook; it will form a wonderful glaze. I like to serve the chicken wings hot but they are equally delicious cold.

20 chicken wings

150ml (1/4 pint) hoisin sauce

Juice of 1 lime

4 tablespoons nam pla (Thai fish sauce)

2 garlic cloves, crushed

1 tablespoon honey

1 tablespoon hot Chinese mustard

2 tablespoons chopped coriander

2 tablespoons mirin (Japanese sweet
  rice wine)

Roasted skate escabeche
with tarragon mustard dressing

Escabeche is a Spanish dish of cooked fish lightly pickled in a piquant marinade. This version uses skate wings, and the marinade is enlivened with tarragon mustard, roasted red and yellow peppers, citrus juice, coriander and capers for a vibrant mix of colours and flavours.

Preheat the oven to 190°C/375°F/gas mark 5. Place the skate wings on a baking tray, brush with half the oil and season with salt and pepper. Roast for 10–12 minutes or until just cooked. Remove from the oven and leave to cool.

Heat the remaining oil in a pan, add the onion and cook over a low heat for 3–4 minutes, until just softened. Add the coriander seeds, chilli and garlic and cook for a further minute.

In a bowl, combine the citrus juices and zest with all the remaining ingredients to make a marinade. Add the softened onion and chilli mixture, then season to taste.

With a sharp knife, carefully remove all the bones from the skate. Add the meat to the marinade, cover and leave in the fridge overnight.

Arrange the fish and marinaded ingredients stacked in a pile, on a large serving platter or individual plates. Drizzle over the marinade juices and serve with lots of crusty bread.

4 x 350g (12oz) prepared skate wings

100ml (3 1/2fl oz) virgin olive oil

1 red onion, thinly sliced

1 teaspoon coriander seeds

1 serrano chilli, thinly sliced

1 garlic clove, crushed

Juice and zest of 1 orange

Juice and zest of 1 lime

Juice and zest of 1 lemon

1 red and 1 yellow pepper, roasted,
  peeled and cut into strips

A handful of coriander leaves

1 tablespoon cocktail capers, rinsed
  and drained

1 teaspoon tarragon mustard

100ml (3 1/2fl oz) dry white wine

90ml (3fl oz) tarragon vinegar

1 tablespoon brown sugar

Salt and freshly ground black pepper

Crispy corn tortillas
with chile con queso and merguez

Heat some vegetable oil in a deep-fat fryer or a large, deep pan to 190°C/375°F and fry the tortilla quarters until crisp and golden. Remove with a slotted spoon and drain on kitchen paper. Keep warm while you prepare the sauce.

Put 2 tablespoons of the frying oil in another pan, add the onion, garlic, tomato, chillies and merguez and cook gently for 5–6 minutes, until the onion is tender. Add the white wine and raise the heat to evaporate it. Reduce the heat again to low, add the cheese and stir until completely melted.

Arrange the tortilla wedges on a flat serving plate and pour over the spicy cheese sauce. Serve immediately.

Vegetable oil for deep-frying

8 x 15cm (6in) corn tortillas, cut into quarters

1 small red onion, finely chopped

2 garlic cloves, crushed

1 tomato, cut into large pieces

4 green jalapeño chillies, deseeded and thinly sliced

100g (4oz) merguez sausage, cut into small dice

100ml (3 1/2 fl oz) dry white wine

175g (6oz) Cheddar cheese, grated

Salmon rillettes
with Asian spices and apple and beetroot relish

Season the salmon with salt and pepper, then steam it until just cooked. Leave to cool completely.

Place the salmon in a bowl and, using a fork, flake the fish into small pieces. Add the curry paste, coriander, ginger and shallots. Bind with the mayonnaise, just to bring it together, then check the seasoning and adjust if necessary.

Place a 6–7.5cm (2 1/2–3in) ring mould or pastry cutter in the centre of a serving plate. Fill the mould with the salmon mixture, level it off with a knife, then carefully remove the mould. Repeat on 3 more serving plates.

For the relish, place the beetroot, apples, ginger and basil in a bowl. In another bowl mix together the lime juice, mustard and oil to form an emulsion, then pour this over the beetroot and apple and mix together gently. Season to taste. Serve with the salmon rillettes.

650g (1lb 7oz) fresh salmon fillet, skinned

2 teaspoons My Curry Paste (see p154)

2 tablespoons chopped coriander

2.5cm (1in) fresh root ginger, finely chopped

2 shallots (or spring onions), finely chopped

4 tablespoons well-flavoured mayonnaise

Salt and freshly ground black pepper

For the apple and beetroot relish:

1 cooked beetroot, shredded

2 Granny Smith apples, peeled, cored and shredded

2.5cm (1in) piece of fresh root ginger, finely shredded

5 basil leaves, shredded

Juice of 1 lime

1/2 teaspoon Dijon mustard

6 tablespoons olive oil

Three-pepper salmon
with grappa, dill and lemon crème fraîche

Mix together the lemon juice and zest, crème fraîche and black pepper. With a sharp carving knife, thinly slice the salmon on the diagonal. Cut a rectangular sheet of greaseproof paper approximately 40 x 20cm (16 x 8in) and brush it liberally with the olive oil. Arrange the salmon slices on the paper, overlapping each slice as you go. Season with salt, then brush over the grappa and sprinkle over the green and pink peppercorns. Scatter over the chopped dill, then top with the crème fraîche, carefully smearing it over the surface with the aid of a palette knife dipped in hot water.

Starting at a long side of the rectangle, carefully roll up the salmon as if making a swiss roll, holding on to the paper, which will be released when the salmon is rolled. Chill for 1 hour.

To serve, cut the roll into 8 slices and place on serving plates. Toss the salad leaves and herbs with the vinaigrette and use to garnish the salmon. Serve with the lemon wedges

HOT TIP To make cracked black pepper, put the peppercorns in a small bowl and break them up roughly with the end of a rolling pin, or use a pestle and mortar.

Juice and zest of 1 lemon

3 tablespoons crème fraîche

1/2 teaspoon black peppercorns, cracked (see Hot Tip)

675g (1 1/2 lb) very fresh salmon fillet, skinned

3 tablespoons olive oil

2 tablespoons grappa

1 teaspoon green peppercorns, lightly crushed with a fork

1 teaspoon pink peppercorns, lightly crushed with a fork

6 tablespoons roughly chopped dill

1 lemon, cut into wedges, to garnish

Salt

For the herb salad:

50g (2oz) frisée lettuce

50g (2oz) young spinach leaves

2 tablespoons each of dill, chervil, chives and basil

2 tablespoons plain vinaigrette of your choice

Balsamic sardines
on crushed mustard potatoes

Heat a non-stick frying pan, then add 2 tablespoons of the oil and fry the sardine fillets for 1 minute on each side, until well seasoned but not coloured. Place the sardine fillets in a large earthenware dish. Add all the remaining ingredients to the pan, bring to the boil and simmer for 10 minutes, then pour this mixture over the fillets. Leave to stand for at least 3 hours, turning the fish at least twice during this time.

Meanwhile, cook the potatoes in a pan of boiling salted water until just tender, then drain and leave until cool enough to handle. Peel the potatoes and place them in a bowl. Crush with a fork until they are chunky, then stir in the olive oil, chilli and Dijon mustard. Finally add the chopped coriander.

To serve, put the warm crushed potatoes on individual serving plates and top with the marinated sardine fillets. Drizzle a little marinade on top.

225ml (7½fl oz) olive oil
8 small sardines, filleted
5 tablespoons white wine vinegar
2 tablespoons balsamic vinegar
1 tablespoon caster sugar
1 small onion, thinly sliced
1 teaspoon black peppercorns
1 teaspoon coriander seeds
1 small dried red chilli
1 fresh bay leaf
1 garlic clove, crushed
For the mustard potatoes:
300g (10oz) new potatoes
100ml (3½fl oz) olive oil
1 red chilli, deseeded and finely chopped
1 teaspoon Dijon mustard
1 tablespoon chopped coriander

Grilled red mullet
with fried tomatoes and rocket gribiche

Here peppery rocket leaves are complemented by a piquant dressing containing capers, gherkins and mustard. Both make a good foil for the oily-textured red mullet.

For the gribiche, separate the egg yolks and the whites and chop the whites into small dice. Put the yolks in a bowl with the mustard and gradually whisk in 100ml (3½fl oz) of the olive oil, as if making mayonnaise. Add the capers, gherkins and egg white, then the parsley and shallots. Heat the vinegar and add to the sauce, then adjust the seasoning. Set aside.

Preheat the grill to its highest setting. Season the fish fillets with salt and pepper and squeeze over a little lemon juice. Arrange on an oiled grill pan, and cook for 2–3 minutes on each side. While the fish is cooking, heat the remaining oil in a frying pan. Add the garlic and cook for 10 seconds to infuse, then add the tomatoes slices and fry for 1 minute on each side, until lightly coloured. Top with the basil, season and remove.

To serve, arrange the tomato slices on individual serving plates and stack 2 red mullet fillets on top. Dress the rocket leaves with the gribiche and place a mound of the salad by the side of the fish. Serve immediately.

2 eggs, hard-boiled
1 teaspoon Dijon mustard
165ml (5½fl oz) olive oil
1½ teaspoons fine capers
1½ teaspoons small gherkins
1 tablespoon chopped parsley
2 shallots, finely chopped
2 tablespoons red wine vinegar
8 x 75g (3oz) red mullet fillets
Lemon juice
2 garlic cloves, crushed
4 beefsteak tomatoes, cut into slices
2 tablespoons roughly chopped basil
A good handful of small rocket leaves
Salt and freshly ground black pepper

Barbecue-spiced squid
with cayenne–blue cheese aïoli

This idea came from a trip to Houston, where I did a promotion at a hotel. The chef took me to a restaurant called Pignetti's, where we drank tequilas all night and the owner brought us a dish of spicy deep-fried squid with a blue cheese sauce. Here is my slightly adapted version – tequilas optional.

First make the aïoli: mix the egg yolks together in a bowl with the garlic, lemon juice and a little salt. Add the oil, drop by drop at first, whisking constantly until the mixture is smooth and thick. Gently mix the blue cheese with 3 tablespoons of hot water to form a paste, then mix into the sauce. Finally add the cayenne pepper and some more salt if needed.

Slice the squid bodies into rings 5mm (1/4in) thick; leave the tentacles in large pieces. Mix together the spice mix, cornflour and baking powder. Heat some vegetable oil in a deep-fat fryer or a large, deep saucepan to 190°C/375°F. Dip the squid pieces in the milk and then in the spice mix, shaking off any excess. Fry in batches in the hot oil for about 1–2 minutes, until brown and crisp; do not overcook or the squid will be tough. Remove the squid and drain on kitchen paper, then sprinkle with salt and Szechuan pepper. Serve immediately, with the aïoli and lemon wedges.

600g (1 1/4 lb) cleaned small or
*   medium squid*
2 tablespoons Barbecue spice mix
*   (see p157)*
100g (4oz) cornflour
1 teaspoon baking powder
Vegetable oil for deep-frying
150ml (1/4 pint) full-fat milk
1 lemon, cut into wedges
Salt and ground Szechuan pepper
For the cayenne–blue cheese aïoli:
2 egg yolks
1 garlic clove, crushed
Juice of 1/2 lemon
175ml (6fl oz) virgin olive oil
75g (3oz) blue cheese
1/4 teaspoon cayenne pepper

HOT TIP The safest way to deep-fry is in a thermostatically controlled deep-fat fryer but you can also use a large, deep saucepan. Never fill it more than a third full with oil and, to avoid the danger of flare-ups, make sure the pan covers the heat source completely. The oil should be hot enough to form bubbles around the food as soon as you put it in. Don't overcrowd the pan, as this will cause the temperature to drop, and remember to dry the food first if necessary, to prevent the oil splattering.

Chargrilled squid fajitas
with spring onions, pepper and rocket

This makes a great snack and is very quick to prepare. Fajitas are soft filled tortillas, usually prepared with meat such as chicken or beef. Squid makes a good light alternative. Serve with your favourite salsa, guacamole and sour cream.

Cook the peppers and spring onions on a ridged grill pan until charred and tender, then remove from the grill and keep warm. Place the squid, including the tentacles, on the grill pan (it should be very hot), season with salt and pepper and grill for 1–2 minutes, turning once.

Shred the squid, peppers and spring onions and place in a bowl. Add the garlic, chilli sauce, lime juice, cumin and rocket and season to taste. Quickly heat the tortillas on the grill for 10 seconds on each side, until slightly charred. arrange the squid and vegetables in the warm tortillas, fold one end of the tortilla over the filling and roll up. Serve immediately.

1 red pepper, halved and deseeded

1 green pepper, halved and deseeded

8 spring onions

4 medium-sized squid, cleaned

1 garlic clove, crushed

6 tablespoons chilli sauce

Juice of 1/2 small lime

1 teaspoon ground cumin

A handful of wild rocket leaves

8 x 15–18cm (6–7in) flour tortillas

Salt and freshly ground black pepper

Roasted mussels
with Indian green chutney

This unusual method of cooking mussels seals in all their natural juices and flavours. It's great served with Grilled black pepper naans (see page 140).

In a blender, blitz together the coriander leaves, ginger, garlic, chillies, cardamom, lemon juice and water to make a smooth paste. Pour into a small bowl and set aside.

In a small frying pan, heat 2 tablespoons of the oil until hot but not smoking. Add the cumin seeds and mustard seeds. When they begin to pop, stir in the turmeric, some salt and the coriander purée. Add another 3 tablespoons of the oil and cook for 1 minute, then remove from the heat.

Preheat the oven to 200°C/400°F/gas mark 6.

Scrub the mussels thoroughly under cold running water, pulling out the beards and discarding any open mussels that do not close when tapped on the work surface. Place the mussels in a baking tin, pour over the remaining oil and mix together. Scatter the coriander stalks on top and place in the oven for 3–4 minutes or until the shells have opened. Remove from the oven and discard the coriander stalks.

Arrange the mussels in a large serving bowl, pour over the chutney and serve immediately.

50g (2oz) coriander leaves (reserve the stalks)

2.5cm (1in) piece of fresh root ginger, chopped

2 garlic cloves, chopped

2 green jalapeño chillies, deseeded and chopped

1/2 teaspoon ground cardamom

Juice of 1 lemon

4 tablespoons water

150ml (1/4 pint) olive oil

1/2 teaspoon cumin seeds

1/2 teaspoon brown mustard seeds

1/2 teaspoon ground turmeric

675g (11/2lb) mussels

Salt and freshly ground black pepper

HOT TIP This versatile chutney can also be stirred into soups or served with vegetables.

✳ Chilled mussels
in harissa salsa

I have very fond memories of my late father, who had an infinite love of seafood, especially mussels. He would eat them at any opportunity, at any time of day, and he taught me to appreciate their delicate qualities, too. Here is one of my favourite ways of serving them, bathed in a spicy vinaigrette. I know he would have loved this recipe.

Scrub the mussels thoroughly under cold running water, pulling out the beards and discarding any open mussels that do not close when tapped on the work surface. Place the mussels in a large saucepan, scatter over the onion, garlic, coriander stalks and chilli flakes, then pour in the wine and enough water just to cover. Put a lid on the pan and place over a high heat to steam for about 5 minutes, or until the mussels have opened, shaking the pan half way through to redistribute the mussels. Drain in a colander, reserving the cooking liquor, and set aside. Strain the liquor through a fine sieve.

For the salsa, mix together all the ingredients in a bowl.

Remove the mussels from their shells but retain half of each shell. Add the warm mussels to the salsa with 4 tablespoons of the strained mussel stock. Leave to cool, then chill for 1 hour.

To serve, place a mussel on each half shell and arrange on a serving dish. Spoon over the salsa and serve at room temperature.

HOT TIP Like all shellfish, mussels must be bought alive. Look for ones that are tightly shut, heavy for their size and smell good. Always discard any with open or broken shells and, if in doubt about their freshness, throw them away. Wrapped in wet newspaper, mussels will keep for up to 2 days in the fridge.

675g (1½lb) very fresh mussels
1 onion, chopped
1 garlic clove, finely sliced
A few coriander stalks
A good pinch of dried red chilli flakes
200ml (7fl oz) dry white wine
For the harissa salsa:
2 plum tomatoes, skinned, deseeded and finely chopped
1 small onion, finely chopped
1 garlic clove, crushed
2 tablespoons chopped coriander
3 tablespoons white wine vinegar
1 tablespoon maple syrup
½teaspoon Harissa (see p156)
Juice of ½ lemon
1 red, 1 green and 1 yellow pepper, roasted, peeled and finely diced

Curried crab tart
with smoky guacamole and mango dressing

Preheat the oven to 200°C/400°F/gas mark 6. In a bowl, combine the crabmeat, mayonnaise, curry paste, cream and chilli. Season to taste, then chill while you prepare the pastry.

Roll out the pastry until it is 5mm (1/4in) thick and then use to line four 8cm (3 1/2 in) loose-bottomed flan tins. Line them with greaseproof paper and fill with baking beans, then bake blind for 5–6 minutes. Remove the beans and paper from the pastry cases and bake for a further 2–3 minutes. Remove from the oven and leave to cool. Reduce the oven temperature to 180°C/350°F/gas mark 4.

Mix together all the ingredients for the mango dressing, season to taste and leave for 15–20 minutes for the flavours to blend.

Put a heaped tablespoon of the guacamole in each of the pastry cases, then top with the crab-meat mixture. Return to the oven to glaze for about 5–6 minutes. Turn the tarts out on to serving plates, place a little of the mango dressing around each one and serve. A little fresh salad goes well with this dish.

300g (10oz) fresh white crabmeat

4 tablespoons well-flavoured mayonnaise

2 teaspoons Red Thai Curry Paste (see p155)

1 tablespoon double cream

1 jalapeño chilli, deseeded and chopped

225g (8oz) shortcrust pastry

4 tablespoons Smoky Guacamole en Molcajete (see p153)

Salt and freshly ground black pepper

For the mango dressing:

1/2 mango, peeled and cut into 5mm (1/4in) dice

2 plum tomatoes, skinned, deseeded and cut into 5mm (1/4in) dice

1 shallot, chopped

Juice of 2 limes

1 tablespoon chopped coriander

1 small serrano chilli, deseeded and chopped

4 tablespoons vegetable oil

Blackened oysters
on spring greens with tomato and horseradish salsa

For the salsa, mix all the ingredients together in a bowl and leave to marinate for up to 1 hour, to allow the flavours to develop.

Shuck the oysters (see Hot Tip below), then wash the shells and set aside.

Remove the stalks from the spring greens, cut the greens into small pieces and wash well. Cook in boiling salted water for 5–6 minutes, then drain thoroughly. Heat 1 tablespoon of the olive oil in a frying pan, add the bacon and fry until crisp. Then add the spring greens and sauté for 2–3 minutes, until tender. Season and keep warm.

Warm the washed oyster shells in a low oven for 5 minutes. Dry the shucked oysters and dredge them with the spice mix. Heat the remaining olive oil in a large frying pan and fry the oysters over a high heat for 30–40 seconds, until they are just cooked and have formed a spicy crust.

Divide the greens and bacon between the heated oyster shells, then put a spicy oyster in each shell and coat with a little salsa. Garnish with the lemon wedges. Serve the remaining salsa separately.

HOT TIP To open oysters you need an oyster knife or a short, strong-bladed knife. Wrap your hand in a tea towel to protect it, then take hold of an oyster and insert the knife blade between the shells, next to the hinge. Twist the knife to lever open the top shell, then cut the muscle connecting the oyster to the shell. Next, loosen the muscle connecting the oyster to the bottom shell and take out the oyster.

20 large rock oysters

350g (12oz) spring greens

4 tablespoons olive oil

100g (4oz) back bacon, chopped

2 tablespoons Blackened Cajun spice mix (see p157)

1 lemon, cut into wedges, to garnish

Salt and freshly ground black pepper

For the tomato and horseradish salsa:

225g (8oz) plum tomatoes, finely diced

1/2 red onion, finely chopped

Juice of 1 lime

2 tablespoons maple syrup

1 red chilli, deseeded and chopped

1 tablespoon coriander leaves

1 teaspoon grated horseradish root

Grilled scallops
with black bean and citrus chilli oil vinaigrette

Mix together all the ingredients for the vinaigrette, then place the scallops in it. Cover with clingfilm and leave in the fridge for 4 hours to marinate.

When ready to serve, heat a ridged grill pan and brush it with a little oil. Remove the scallops from the vinaigrette and place on the grill to cook for 30 seconds on each side. Arrange on serving plates.

Remove the coriander sprigs from the vinaigrette and, using a slotted spoon, spoon the vinaigrette ingredients over the scallops. Drizzle over a little of the liquid and garnish with fresh coriander leaves. Serve immediately.

8 medium-large scallops, cleaned

A little oil for grilling

Coriander leaves, to garnish

For the vinaigrette:

Juice and zest of 2 oranges

Juice and zest of 4 limes

1 teaspoon finely chopped fresh ginger

2 garlic cloves, thinly sliced

4 spring onions, shredded

75g (3oz) cooked black beans

2 plum tomatoes, skinned, deseeded and diced

4 tablespoons Chilli oil (see p152)

1 green jalapeño chilli, thinly sliced

1/4 teaspoon smoked paprika

4 sprigs of coriander

Devilled scallops
in bacon with garlic–pea purée and sage butter

Devilling is a good old-fashioned British technique, using Worcestershire sauce, mustard or cayenne to spice up foods such as bloaters, chicken and crab. Here, scallops are given a generous dusting of cayenne pepper to make a favourite dish of mine.

Preheat the oven to 200°C/400°F/gas mark 6. Place the unpeeled garlic cloves on a baking tray, pour over the oil and roast for 15–20 minutes, until lightly charred and very soft. Remove from the oven and leave to cool. Squeeze the garlic flesh out of its skin and place in a blender.

Cook the peas in boiling salted water until very tender, then drain well and add to the blender with 25g (1oz) of the butter. Season with salt and pepper and blitz until smooth and silky in texture. Keep warm.

Dust the scallops well with the cayenne pepper and a little salt, then wrap in the bacon and secure with a cocktail stick. Place under a hot grill or on a ridged grill pan for 2–3 minutes on each side, until the bacon is crisp and the scallops just cooked.

To serve, place a little mound of pea purée on each serving plate and top with a scallop. Keep warm. Heat a small frying pan until very hot, then add the remaining butter and cook until foaming and nutty in fragrance.

Add the sage leaves and lemon juice, then pour the foaming butter over and around the scallops and serve immediately.

5 garlic cloves

3 tablespoons olive oil

175g (6oz) frozen peas

150g (5oz) unsalted butter

4 very large sea scallops (or 8 medium-sized ones), cleaned, coral removed

1 teaspoon cayenne pepper

8 back bacon rashers

10 small sage leaves

Juice of 1/2 lemon

Salt and freshly ground black pepper

Black sesame lobster tempura
with Japanese slaw and wasabi vinaigrette

This intriguing dish may sound complicated but in fact there's very little cooking involved. The Japanese slaw is cool and refreshing, and adds a wonderful crunch to the deep-fried lobster.

Cut each lobster tail in half down the centre but leave the claws whole.

In a bowl, whisk together the eggs and water until pale and foamy. Add the bicarbonate of soda and flour and mix lightly to make a batter. It should remain a little lumpy.

For the vinaigrette, place the ginger and wasabi paste in a bowl, then whisk in the rice vinegar, mirin and soy sauce. Whisk in the oil a little at a time to form an emulsion. Stir in the hot water. Add all the ingredients for the slaw and mix well together. Leave for 10–15 minutes to allow the flavours to meld.

Heat some vegetable oil in a deep-fat fryer or a large, deep pan to 180°C/350°F. Dip the lobster tails and claws in the tempura batter, sprinkle liberally with the sesame seeds and fry for 2–3 minutes or until crisp. Remove and drain on kitchen paper. Put the lobster on 4 serving plates, one half tail and one claw per person, garnish with a heap of coleslaw and drizzle over any remaining dressing, then serve immediately.

2 x 675g (1½lb) lobsters, cooked, shell removed

2 eggs

125ml (4fl oz) iced water

A good pinch of bicarbonate of soda

75g (3oz) plain flour

Vegetable oil for deep-frying

1½ teaspoons black sesame seeds

For the wasabi vinaigrette:

5cm (2in) piece of fresh root ginger, finely grated

½ teaspoon wasabi paste

2 tablespoons rice vinegar

2 tablespoons mirin (Japanese sweet rice wine)

1 teaspoon light soy sauce

125ml (4fl oz) vegetable oil

2 tablespoons hot water

For the slaw:

1 carrot, finely shredded

50g (2oz) red cabbage, finely shredded

75g celeriac, finely shredded

50g (2oz) beansprouts

50g (2oz) arame or hijiki seaweed

HOT TIP The wasabi vinaigrette can also be served with carpaccio of beef or as a dressing for a meat salad.

Marinated goat's cheese
with nectarine and honey peppercorn dressing

Mix together all the marinade ingredients in a small dish, then add the goat's cheese. Cover and refrigerate for at least 4 hours or, better still, overnight. Transfer the cheeses to a small baking dish and strain the oil through a fine sieve; you will need 5 tablespoons of it for the dressing.

For the dressing, crush the pink peppercorns in a bowl, then add the mustard and honey and blend together. Whisk in a tablespoon of the reserved marinade to form an emulsion, then whisk in the vinegar, followed by 4 tablespoons of the mari-nade. Add the hot water and adjust the seasoning.

Warm the goat's cheese under a hot grill or in a moderate oven for 2–3 minutes, until just heated through, but do not let it melt. To serve, place the spinach leaves in a bowl with the walnuts and nectarine slices, drizzle over the pink peppercorn dressing and season lightly. Put the cheeses on individual serving plates and sprinkle with some lightly crushed pink peppercorns, then garnish with a mound of salad and serve. Good crusty bread makes an ideal accompaniment to this dish.

4 crottins de Chavignol (or use a 350g/ 12oz goat's cheese log, sliced into quarters)

1 bag of young spinach leaves

2 tablespoons walnut halves

1 ripe but firm nectarine, stoned and thinly sliced

Salt and freshly ground black pepper

For the marinade:

150ml (1/4 pint) olive oil

2 garlic cloves, crushed

1 bay leaf

1/2 teaspoon thyme leaves

1/2 teaspoon rosemary

For the dressing:

1 teaspoon pink peppercorns, plus extra to garnish

1/2 teaspoon Dijon mustard

1 teaspoon honey

1 tablespoon white wine vinegar

1 tablespoon hot water

HOT TIP If you are weight conscious, replace half the oil in the dressing with reduced chicken stock.

fish and seafood

Roast cod on smoked salmon
and cabbage hash with horseradish butter

Bring a large pan of water to the boil, add a little salt, then add the shredded cabbage and bring back to the boil. Reduce the heat to a simmer and cook for 5–8 minutes. Drain off most of the water, leaving only a little in the pan. Add the caraway seeds and cream and cook over a gentle heat for about 5 minutes, until the cabbage is well cooked and just bound by the cream. Adjust the seasoning and stir in the smoked salmon. Keep warm.

Heat a large frying pan, add the oil and 25g (1oz) of the butter, then fry the cod, skin-side first, for 3–4 minutes per side, until golden and crisp. When it is done, divide the cabbage between 4 serving plates, top with a crisp piece of cod and sprinkle over a little sea salt.

Heat a small frying pan, melt the remaining butter in it, then add the lemon juice and finally the horseradish. Pour the sauce over the cod and cabbage hash and serve immediately, with plain mashed potatoes.

1/2 white or pale green cabbage, finely shredded

1 teaspoon caraway seeds

2 tablespoons double cream

75g (3oz) smoked salmon, shredded

4 tablespoons olive oil

100g (4oz) unsalted butter

4 x 200g (7oz) cod fillets (skin on)

Juice of 1/2 lemon

11/2 teaspoons finely grated horse-radish root

Sea salt and freshly ground black pepper

Pepper-grilled swordfish
with preserved lemon oil and wilted chard

Swordfish is fairly robust, so I like to treat it in the same way as meat occasionally – here it is coated with black pepper, like a steak. Swiss chard makes the ideal accompaniment but if you can't get hold of any, you could always use spinach instead.

Heat half the oil in a small pan, add the garlic and tomatoes and cook over a low heat for 2 minutes. Stir in the dried chilli, preserved lemons and lemon juice and zest, then remove from the heat and leave to infuse.

Heat another 3 tablespoons of the oil in a pan, add the chard and cook over a low heat for 10–15 minutes, until wilted. Season to taste and keep warm while you cook the fish.

Heat a grill to its highest setting. Coat the swordfish steaks with the remaining oil, then coat both sides of the fish with the cracked peppercorns and season with a little salt. Grill for 2–3 minutes on each side. Place each steak on a bed of the Swiss chard, coat with the lemon and tomato dressing and serve immediately.

HOT TIP Preserved lemons are a staple of Moroccan cuisine, typically used in tagines or in fish dishes such as this one. When a recipe calls for preserved lemon, use the rind only, as the flesh tastes too briny.

150ml (1/4 pint) olive oil
1 garlic clove, crushed
4 plum tomatoes, skinned, deseeded
*   and cut into small dice*
1/2 teaspoon dried red chilli flakes
1 tablespoon finely chopped salted
*   preserved lemons (see Hot Tip)*
Juice and zest of 1 lemon
350g (12oz) Swiss chard, coarsely
*   shredded*
4 x 175g (6oz) swordfish steaks
1 teaspoon coarsely cracked black
*   peppercorns (see Hot Tip on p28)*
Salt and freshly ground black pepper

Smoked mackerel fishcakes
with horseradish mayo

For the horseradish mayo, mix all the ingredients together and season to taste.

Mix the smoked mackerel with the mashed potatoes, egg yolks, dill and anchovy essence and season to taste. Chill the mixture until firm enough to handle, then, on a floured surface, shape it into flat cakes, using floured hands and a palette knife.

In a shallow bowl, lightly whisk the egg whites to break them up. Spread the flour out on one large plate and the breadcrumbs on another. Dip the fishcakes in the flour, then in the egg white and finally in the breadcrumbs. Shallow-fry them in a little hot oil until golden brown, turning once.

Serve with the horseradish mayo.

450g (1lb) smoked mackerel, flaked
450g (1lb) mashed potatoes
2 eggs, separated
1 tablespoon chopped dill
1 teaspoon anchovy essence
50g (2oz) plain flour
75g (3oz) fresh white breadcrumbs
Vegetable oil for shallow-frying
Salt and freshly ground black pepper
For the horseradish mayo:
125g (41/2oz) good-quality mayonnaise
1 tablespoon grated horseradish root
1 tablespoon chopped dill
1 tablespoon grain mustard
A dash of wine vinegar
1 teaspoon lemon juice

* Jerk mackerel
with jollof rice and Caribbean mojo

The Caribbean term, jerk, originally referred to marinated meats that were covered with ashes and cooked slowly in a pit. Today it can mean a seasoning mixture, the style of cooking or the finished dish. The spice rub in this recipe is based on traditional Jamaican jerk seasoning. It is great rubbed on just about any meat or fish before grilling. You can also buy jerk sauces or seasoning powders.

Jollof is a gently spiced tomato-flavoured rice. I picked up the recipe for it when I was working in the Caribbean.

Make 3 deep slashes through the skin on each side of the mackerel pieces and season with salt. Put 2 tablespoons of the olive oil in a bowl, add the thyme, spices, sugar, spring onions and Worcestershire sauce and mix well. Smear this mixture all over the mackerel and leave to marinate for 1 hour.

Meanwhile prepare the jollof rice: heat the butter in a large saucepan, add the onion, garlic and all-spice and sweat over a moderate heat until softened. Add the rice and cook for 1 minute, until the butter is absorbed – do not brown. Stir in the tomato purée, then pour in the stock, season to taste and bring to the boil. Reduce the heat and cook gently until all the liquid has been absorbed and the rice is tender.

Preheat the grill to its highest setting. Clean the mackerel of any excess marinade, then place it on a grill pan. Pour over the remaining oil and grill about 15–20cm (6–8in) from the heat for 10–12 minutes or until browned and cooked through. Serve on the jollof rice with the Caribbean mojo.

2 x 675g (1½lb) cleaned mackerel, head and tail removed, fish cut in half crosswise

5 tablespoons olive oil

1 teaspoon dried thyme

1 teaspoon ground allspice

1/4 teaspoon grated nutmeg

1/4 teaspoon ground cinnamon

1 tablespoon freshly ground black pepper

1/2 teaspoon dried red chilli flakes

1/2 teaspoon sugar

6 spring onions, finely chopped

1 teaspoon Worcestershire sauce

1 quantity of Caribbean mojo (see p151)

Salt and freshly ground black pepper

For the jollof rice:

50g (2oz) unsalted butter

1/2 onion, chopped

3 garlic cloves, crushed

1/2 teaspoon ground allspice

225g (8oz) long grain rice

1 tablespoon tomato purée

450ml (3/4 pint) chicken stock (or water)

Fried baby sole
with banana, flaked almonds and devilled sauce

There is a classic dish called Sole Caprice, consisting of fried sole, mango chutney, banana and sauce Robert, which I've always loved. Here's a lighter, fresher version that retains all the charm of the original.

For the sauce, melt 10g (1/4oz) of the butter in a pan, add the shallots and peppercorns and sweat until softened. Add the thyme and bay leaf. Pour in the wine and vinegar and bring to the boil, then add the stock and simmer until the sauce has reduced by half its volume. Cut the remaining butter into cubes and whisk into the sauce a little at a time. Strain through a fine sieve and season to taste with cayenne pepper and salt. Keep warm while you prepare the fish.

Season the fish fillets liberally with salt and pepper. Mix the coriander and panko crumbs together. Dip the fillets in the melted butter, then in the coriander crumbs. Heat the oil in a large frying pan and then add 2 tablespoons of the melted butter. Carefully add the fish fillets and cook for 2–3 minutes on each side, until golden. Keep warm.

Heat the remaining butter in a separate frying pan, add the bananas and brown sugar and cook until lightly caramelised. Season the sauce lightly with salt and pepper.

To serve, place a tablespoon of mango chutney on each serving plate and top with 4 fillets of sole. Then arrange the caramelised bananas and flaked almonds on top and pour a little of the devilled sauce around the fish.

*Skinned fillets from 4 x 350–400g
  (12–14oz) baby sole*
2 tablespoons chopped coriander
*100g (4oz) panko crumbs (see Hot Tip on
  p47) or dried white breadcrumbs*
100g (4oz) unsalted butter, melted
4 tablespoons vegetable oil
*3 bananas, peeled and cut on the
  diagonal into slices 1cm (1/2in) thick*
1 teaspoon brown sugar
4 tablespoons mango chutney
2 tablespoons flaked almonds, toasted
Salt and freshly ground black pepper

For the devilled sauce:

50g (2oz) cold unsalted butter
2 shallots, finely chopped
6 black peppercorns, crushed
1 sprig of thyme
1 small bay leaf
5 tablespoons dry white wine
5 tablespoons white wine vinegar
150ml (1/4 pint) meat stock
A pinch of cayenne pepper

Sea bass
with devilled crab and red pepper chutney

Ideally, the chutney should be made at least 3 days in advance to give the flavours time to mellow.

For the chutney, sweat the onion and garlic in the oil for 4–5 minutes, until softened but not coloured. Add the roasted peppers, ginger and chilli and cook for 5 minutes, then stir in the vinegar and brown sugar and cook for another 5 minutes. Add the raisins and passata and simmer for 20 minutes, until the chutney is very reduced and syrupy. Remove from the heat and leave to cool.

Cut the bass fillets in half to obtain 4 nice bass supremes. Mix together the crabmeat, mayonnaise, chillies, ginger, mace and coriander, then stir in the breadcrumbs and season with salt and pepper. Spoon the mixture on top of each bass fillet in a layer about 5mm (1/4in) thick. Place in the fridge until needed.

For the sauce, put the chicken stock, ginger and lemongrass in a pan and simmer for 10–15 minutes, until reduced by one third in volume. Whisk in the olive oil, season to taste and then strain through a fine sieve. Keep warm.

Preheat the oven to 230°C/450°F/gas mark 8. Heat 2 tablespoons of the olive oil in a large pan, add the spinach and cook for 2–3 minutes, until wilted. Season and drain well.

Heat the remaining oil in a large ovenproof frying pan over a high heat. Add the bass fillets and leave until sealed underneath, then transfer to the oven to cook through and crisp up the crab topping. To serve, divide the spinach between 4 shallow soup plates, top with the baked bass, garnish with a spoonful of chutney, then pour a little of the sauce lightly around the bass.

HOT TIP Panko crumbs are dried breadcrumbs used in oriental cooking, especially for deep-fried dishes. They can be hard to obtain but it's worth trying to find them, since they give a fantastic crisp texture. Ordinary dried white breadcrumbs can, of course, be substituted.

1 x 1.3kg (3lb) sea bass, filleted

350g (12oz) fresh white crabmeat

3 tablespoons well-flavoured mayonnaise

1 red serrano chilli, deseeded and chopped

1 green jalapeño chilli, deseeded and chopped

1/2 teaspoon ground mace

2 tablespoons chopped coriander leaves

6 tablespoons panko crumbs (see Hot Tip) or dried white breadcrumbs

5 tablespoons olive oil

450g (1lb) fresh spinach

Salt and freshly ground black pepper

For the red pepper chutney:

1 onion, chopped

2 garlic cloves, crushed

1 tablespoon olive oil

2 roasted red peppers, peeled and cut into strips 1cm (1/2in) thick

1 teaspoon finely chopped fresh root ginger

1 teaspoon deseeded and finely chopped New Mexican chilli

100ml (3 1/2fl oz) red wine vinegar

50g (2oz) brown sugar

25g (1oz) raisins

100ml (3 1/2fl oz) tomato passata

For the sauce:

200ml (7fl oz) well-flavoured chicken stock

2.5cm (1in) piece of fresh root ginger, grated

2 lemongrass stalks, outer layers removed, shredded

3 tablespoons olive oil

Roasted salmon
with fennel, courgette and romesco sauce

Until relatively recently, salmon was an expensive fish. Now it's cheap enough to use often, and I love experimenting with it. Spices go well with salmon because they cut the richness. Here the tangy bite of the Spanish romesco sauce is a particularly good match.

For the romesco sauce, soak the roasted chillies in hot water for 30 minutes, then drain. Put the tomatoes in a saucepan and cook over a moderate heat until almost all the liquid has evaporated. Remove from the heat and leave to cool. Place the chilli, roasted pepper, garlic, tomato purée, almonds and bread in a blender, add the tomatoes and blitz until smooth. Slowly add the lemon juice and oil while the machine is running. Season to taste.

Place the salmon fillets in a shallow dish. Mix the oil, herb stalks and garlic together and pour them over the salmon, then leave to marinate at room temperature for 1 hour.

Preheat the oven to 200°C/400°F/gas mark 6.

Place the fennel in a large saucepan, cover with water and bring to the boil. Simmer for 4–5 minutes, until tender, then drain. Heat an ovenproof frying pan, clean the marinated salmon of its herbs and fry, skin-side up, for 1 minute or until golden. Turn it over, then place in the oven to roast for 5–8 minutes, until crisp.

Meanwhile, heat the butter in a frying pan, add the courgettes and fry for 4–5 minutes until lightly golden. Add the fennel and black olives and season to taste.

Arrange the vegetables on 4 serving plates, top with the roasted salmon and pour over the romesco sauce. Garnish with the fresh herbs.

4 x 150g (5oz) salmon fillets (skin on)
4 tablespoons olive oil
1 tablespoon coriander leaves (reserve the stalks)
1 tablespoon small basil leaves (reserve the stalks)
1 garlic clove, crushed
8 baby fennel bulbs, trimmed
50g (2oz) unsalted butter
2 courgettes, thickly sliced
8 black olives, stoned and halved
Salt and freshly ground black pepper

For the romesco sauce:
2 dried De Arbol chillies, roasted (see p8)
200g (7oz) ripe tomatoes, skinned, deseeded and coarsely chopped
1 red pepper, roasted, peeled and chopped
2 garlic cloves, crushed
2 teaspoons tomato purée
40g (1½oz) blanched almonds, toasted
1 slice of white bread, crusts removed
2 tablespoons lemon juice
5 tablespoons olive oil

Chilli-roasted salmon
crisp vegetables and fragrant coconut rice

Preheat the oven to 180°C/350°F/gas mark 4. First prepare the dressing by mixing all the ingredients together. Set aside.

Dust the salmon liberally with the chilli powder and some salt. Heat a little oil in an ovenproof frying pan, place the salmon in it skin-side down and cook for 1 minute. Turn the fish over, transfer to the oven and cook for 4–5 minutes, until just done.

Heat the cooked rice in a pan with the lemongrass and coconut cream, then season to taste. Pack into 4 buttered ramekins and keep warm.

For the vegetables, heat the butter and sesame oil in a large frying pan, add all the vegetables and the garlic and stir-fry for 2–3 minutes, until crisp.

To serve, unmould the rice timbales on to 4 individual serving plates and top with the salmon. Arrange the stir-fried vegetables on top. Mix all the ingredients for the dressing together until the mixture is creamy. Pour around the salmon and serve immediately.

4 x 175g (6oz) salmon fillets (skin on)

2 tablespoons chilli powder

A little oil for frying

150g (5oz) cooked basmati rice

2 lemongrass stalks, outer layers removed, very finely chopped

100ml (3 1/2fl oz) unsweetened coconut cream

Salt and freshly ground black pepper

For the dressing:

2 tablespoons light soy sauce

2 shallots, finely chopped

4 tablespoons rice vinegar

4 teaspoons sesame oil

1 tablespoon sugar

1cm (1/2in) piece of fresh root ginger, finely chopped

1 1/2 small red chillies, deseeded and chopped

2 tablespoons chopped coriander

For the crisp vegetables:

25g (1oz) butter

2 tablespoons sesame oil

1/4 red pepper, cut into thin strips

1/4 yellow pepper, cut into thin strips

1 small pak choi, shredded

6 red radishes, thinly sliced

50g (2oz) beansprouts

100g (4oz) shiitake mushrooms, quartered

1 garlic clove, crushed

Grilled salmon trout
with a horseradish crust and beetroot vinaigrette

These crisp salmon trout fillets are accompanied by grilled courgettes and leeks here but I also like to serve them on a bed of creamy mashed potato flavoured with puréed sweetcorn.

Cover the salmon trout fillets with a large piece of clingfilm and lightly flatten them out into neat escalopes about 1cm (1/2in) thick, using a meat bat or a rolling pin.

In a shallow container, mix together the horseradish, smoked salmon, dill, breadcrumbs and a little salt and pepper. Season the salmon trout escalopes with salt and pepper and squeeze over a little lemon juice. Dip the escalopes into the melted butter, then into the breadcrumb mixture on one side. Brush off any excess crumbs, then place in a well-buttered grill pan, crumb-side up. Chill until required.

For the dressing, mix all the ingredients together and season to taste.

Preheat the grill to a medium setting (or use a ridged grill pan). Toss the courgettes and leeks with the oil and some seasoning and cook them under the grill until golden and tender. Keep warm. Place the salmon trout under the grill to cook for about 3–4 minutes, until the crumbs are crisp and golden in colour.

To serve, put the grilled courgettes and leeks on 4 serving plates, top with the salmon trout and pour around the dressing.

4 x 175g (6oz) salmon trout fillets, skinned

2 tablespoons grated horseradish root

50g (2oz) smoked salmon, very finely chopped

1 tablespoon chopped dill

100g (4oz) panko crumbs (see Hot Tip on p47) or dried white breadcrumbs

Lemon juice

75g (3oz) unsalted butter, melted

2 courgettes, cut into slices 5mm (1/4in) thick

12 baby leeks, trimmed

4 tablespoons olive oil

Salt and freshly ground black pepper

For the beetroot vinaigrette:

1 red pepper, roasted, peeled and finely diced

1 small beetroot, cooked, peeled and finely diced

1 shallot, finely diced

Zest of 1/2 lemon

1 tablespoon superfine capers, rinsed and drained

1/4 teaspoon saffron strands, steeped in 2 tablespoons boiling water

1 tablespoon chopped dill

6 tablespoons plain vinaigrette dressing of your choice

Chilli-salt-baked red mullet
with orange–paprika oil

This simple-tasting dish is good served on a fresh tomato salad or with buttery couscous. Baking the mullet in salt seals in all the wonderful juices, so it emerges moist and succulent.

Preheat the oven to 200°C/400°F/gas mark 6. Place a layer of about half the chilli salt in a large baking tin and put the cleaned mullet on top. Sprinkle over the rosemary and lay 1 bay leaf on each fish. Completely cover the mullet with the remaining chilli salt and then bake for 25 minutes.

Meanwhile mix all the ingredients for the oil together until you have a smooth emulsion. Remove the fish from the oven and leave to rest for 5 minutes. Carefully remove the salt from around the fish and discard. Transfer the mullet to a serving dish and drizzle over the oil.

HOT TIP In Indonesia and Malaysia, chilli salt is available ready prepared. It is well worth trying to find some here but it is also very simple to prepare at home. Just toast 10 De Arbol chillies in a hot frying pan for 20 seconds to release their fragrance. Place in a spice mill or coffee grinder and blitz to a fine powder, then mix with 450g (1lb) fine sea salt. Store in an airtight container for about a week before using, so the salt becomes permeated with the chilli.

450g (1lb) chilli salt (see Hot Tip)

4 x 400g (14oz) red mullet, cleaned, fins and tails removed

4 rosemary sprigs, roughly chopped

4 bay leaves

For the orange–paprika oil:

100ml (3½fl oz) virgin olive oil

2 teaspoons hot Hungarian paprika

1 tablespoon coriander leaves

Juice of 2 oranges and zest of 1

2 teaspoons Harissa (see p156)

Salt and freshly ground black pepper

Asian blackened monkfish
with pickled vegetables and mint labna

This dish combines Eastern spicing with monkfish and labna, a Middle Eastern yoghurt cheese. The minted cheese is cool and refreshing against the fiery heat of the pickled vegetables. The vegetables also make a wonderful vegetarian dish served with rice.

For the labna, line a small sieve with a double layer of dampened muslin and put it over a bowl. Put the yoghurt in the sieve, then tie up the ends of the muslin and leave overnight to drain. The next day, mix the yoghurt with the lemon and mint.

For the pickled vegetables, heat half the oil in a deep frying pan, add all the vegetables and fry until golden. Remove from the pan and drain well. Heat the remaining oil in a heavy-based saucepan, throw in the cumin, fenugreek and curry leaves and remove from the heat. After 1 minute, add the garlic and chilli powder and return to the heat. Now add the tomato purée, a little salt and pepper and the fried vegetables. Reduce the heat and cook for 5–10 minutes, then stir in the sugar and vinegar. Remove from the heat and keep warm.

Season the fish liberally with the spice mix. Heat the oil in a large frying pan, then add the butter. Sear the fish in the hot fat on all sides for about 5–8 minutes, until golden brown.

To serve, divide the pickled vegetables between 4 serving plates, and place in a mound. Arrange the monkfish on top, then pour the labna around the fish.

4 x 175g (6oz) monkfish fillets

4 tablespoons Asian blackened spice
   mix (p156)

3 tablespoons olive oil

50g (2oz) unsalted butter

For the mint labna:

150ml (1/4 pint) yoghurt

Juice and zest of 1/4 lemon

1 tablespoon chopped mint

For the pickled vegetables:

125ml (4fl oz) vegetable oil

1 sweet potato, peeled and cut into
   5mm (1/4in) dice

50g (2oz) button onions, peeled

1 small cauliflower, cut into small florets

1 courgette, cut into 5mm (1/4in) dice

1/2 teaspoon cumin seeds

1/4 teaspoon fenugreek seeds

2 curry leaves, shredded

2 garlic cloves, crushed

1 teaspoon chilli powder

1 tablespoon tomato purée

A pinch of sugar

4 tablespoons vinegar

Salt and freshly ground black pepper

HOT TIP The pickled vegetables can be prepared in advance and kept in the fridge for 2–3 days, or longer if you bottle them in a sterilised jar. However, they will become spicier. Since I love hot food, I prefer them this way – the choice is yours!

Parsee monkfish curry
with mashed lentils and poppadom chips

The Parsees originate from Persia but settled in Bombay over a thousand years ago. Their cooking has a distinctive character, with hot/sour/sweet combinations and plenty of chillies. The sauces tend to be thick and savoury, and very fragrant.

Place the garlic and ginger in a blender with 100ml (3 1/2 fl oz) of water and blitz to a paste. Heat a small frying pan over a high heat, add the whole spices and chilli flakes and toast them for 1 minute to release their fragrance. Place in a spice mill or coffee grinder and blitz to a fine powder. Add the turmeric and ground cloves and set aside.

Heat the vegetable oil in a large frying pan, then add the onion and fry until golden. Add the garlic-ginger paste and cook for 2 minutes, then stir in the ground spices. Add the monkfish and cook for 2–3 minutes. Stir in the tomatoes and 300ml (1/2 pint) of water and bring to the boil.

Cover and simmer for 5–8 minutes, then remove the monkfish with a slotted spoon.

Add the cooked lentils, sugar and lemon juice to the pan and cook for 10–15 minutes, then mash the lentils with a spoon to give a chunky texture. Stir in the coconut milk and return the monkfish to the sauce. Cook for a further 10 minutes, then adjust the seasoning and garnish with the freshly chopped mint and coriander.

To make the poppadom chips, cut the poppadoms into 5cm (2in) pieces, arrange them on a plate and place in a microwave for about 1 minute.

Serve the chips immediately, with the fish curry.

2 garlic cloves, peeled
2.5cm (1in) piece of fresh root ginger
1 teaspoon cumin seeds
1/2 teaspoon cardamom seeds
1/2 teaspoon black peppercorns
1 teaspoon dried red chilli flakes
1 teaspoon ground turmeric
1/2 teaspoon ground cloves
4 tablespoons vegetable oil
1 onion, finely chopped
675g (1 1/2lb) monkfish tail fillet, cut
  into 5cm (2in) pieces
200g (7oz) canned tomatoes, crushed
300g (10oz) cooked red lentils
1 teaspoon dark brown sugar
Juice of 1/2 lemon
100ml (3 1/2 fl oz) coconut milk
Chopped mint and coriander, to garnish
8 spicy poppadoms
Salt and freshly ground black pepper

Spicy Moroccan sea bream
with garlic, raisin and almond stuffing

This stuffing is sweet and moist, with a little spiciness typical of Moroccan cooking. In true Moroccan tradition, I have used raisins here but I have also tried it with dates, which worked equally well.

For the stuffing, cook the rice in a pan of boiling salted water for 45–50 minutes or until tender. Drain in a colander and leave to cool. Heat the butter in a large pan, add the onion and garlic and cook over a low heat until softened. Raise the heat, add the cooked rice, allspice and harissa and toss to coat the rice with the spices. Cook for 2–3 minutes, stir-frying the mixture a little. Place in a bowl, add the raisins, pine kernels, ground almonds and coriander and leave to cool.

Stir in the beaten egg and season to taste. **Preheat** the oven to 200°C/400°F/gas mark 6. Slash the fish 3 times on each side and then season inside and outside with salt and pepper. Fill the cavity with the spicy rice stuffing, packing it in well, then place the fish in a large baking tin, squeeze over the lemon juice and pour over the oil. Place in the oven for 20–25 minutes, until the fish is cooked. Serve with a little olive oil drizzled over the fish and accompanied by the lemon wedges.

HOT TIP With its wonderful colour, Camargue red rice is definitely destined to be a fashionable ingredient. It is an unpolished wholegrain rice from the Camargue area of France. You should be able to find it in large supermarkets and delicatessens.

1 x 1.3kg (3lb) sea bream, cleaned and
   gutted
Juice of 1 lemon
6 tablespoons olive oil, plus a little extra
   to serve
1 lemon, cut into wedges
Salt and freshly ground black pepper
For the stuffing:
150g (5oz) Camargue red rice (see Hot
   Tip), washed
50g (2oz) unsalted butter
1 onion, finely chopped
2 garlic cloves, crushed
1/2 teaspoon ground allspice
1 teaspoon Harissa (see p156)
100g (4oz) raisins, soaked in a little hot
   water for 20 minutes and then drained
50g (2oz) pine kernels, toasted
2 tablespoons ground almonds
4 tablespoons chopped coriander
1 egg, lightly beaten

Cajun turbot
with wilted greens, butternut squash and Creole vinaigrette

This wonderful mustardy vinaigrette is very versatile. I like to use it on leaf salads or tossed with hot vegetables such as French beans or tomatoes.

For the Creole vinaigrette mix all the ingredients together and leave to stand for at least 30 minutes before use.

Heat the butter and half the oil in a large frying pan and add the squash, mixed greens and 4 table-spoons of water. Cover and cook over a high heat for about 8–10 minutes, until the vegetables are tender. Add the sweetcorn and heat through briefly. Season with salt and pepper and keep warm while you prepare the fish.

Dust the turbot fillets all over with the spice mix. Heat the remaining oil in a large frying pan over a high heat and add the turbot (it will give off a fair amount of smoke, which is indicative of a black-ened dish). Cook until well browned, then turn the fish over and cook the other side. It will take about 4–5 minutes altogether, depending on thickness.

Arrange the vegetables on serving plates, top with the turbot and pour the Creole vinaigrette around. Serve immediately.

HOT TIP When buying turbot fillet, always check that the flesh is not bruised. If it is, this indicates that the fish has not been bled properly, in which case it is unusable.

25g (1oz) unsalted butter

4 tablespoons olive oil

1/2 butternut squash, peeled, deseeded and cut into wedges 5–10mm (1/4–1/2in) thick

675g (1½lb) young mixed greens, such as kale, mustard greens, Swiss chard and spinach

100g (4oz) canned sweetcorn, drained

4 x 175g (6oz) turbot fillets

4 tablespoons Blackened Cajun spice mix (see p157)

Salt and freshly ground black pepper

For the Creole vinaigrette:

2 tablespoons red wine vinegar

125ml (4fl oz) olive oil

2 teaspoons coarse grain mustard

2 shallots, finely chopped

1 red jalapeño chilli, deseeded and finely diced

1 red pepper, roasted, peeled and finely diced

1 teaspoon lemon juice

Chargrilled John Dory
with tomatoes, fennel and chilli and rocket salsa verde

John Dory can be difficult to find unless you are lucky enough to have a good-quality fishmonger locally. It is best during the late summer and early autumn, which is the ideal time to prepare this light and simple dish. If you do have a problem obtaining it, replace it with sole, turbot or brill.

Warm the virgin olive oil in a shallow saucepan, add the fennel and bay leaf and leave barely simmering for 10–15 minutes, until the fennel is just tender. Add the garlic cloves, tomato quarters and olives and leave to cook for a further 10 minutes.

Meanwhile, in a blender or food processor, blend all the ingredients for the salsa verde together. Season to taste and set aside. Heat a ridged grill pan. Season the fish with cayenne, salt and pepper and cook on the grill for 3–4 minutes each side.

Drain the fennel and tomato mixture and place on 4 serving plates, then top with the chargrilled fish. Put the balsamic vinegar and meat stock in a small pan and bring to the boil, then whisk in 2 tablespoons of the oil from cooking the vegetables. Adjust the seasoning.

To serve, top the fish with a spoonful of the spicy salsa verde and pour a little of the sauce around.

100ml (3 1/2 fl oz) virgin olive oil

2 fennel bulbs, trimmed and cut into wedges

1 bay leaf

8 garlic cloves, peeled

8 plum tomatoes, quartered

12 green olives, stoned

900g (2lb) John Dory fillet, skinned and cut into 12 fingers

A pinch of cayenne pepper

2 tablespoons balsamic vinegar

100ml (3 1/2 fl oz) meat stock

Salt and freshly ground black pepper

For the salsa verde:

4 tablespoons rocket leaves

2 tablespoons basil leaves

2 tablespoons flat-leaf parsley

40g (1 1/2 oz) superfine capers, rinsed and drained

1 garlic clove, crushed

1 tablespoon balsamic vinegar

1 tablespoon Dijon mustard

1 green jalapeño chilli, deseeded and chopped

4 tablespoons olive oil

Adobado grilled snapper
with curly fennel and radish ceviche

Adobado is the Mexican term for a meat or fish dish that has been marinated in a punchy, spicy-sour mixture. It should not be confused with an adobo, which uses a similar marinade but is more of a stew.

For the ceviche, I like to use my favourite oriental radishes, which are a stunning red or green colour. Available in Chinese grocer's shops, they are well worth seeking out. Mooli (daikon) or ordinary red radishes may be substituted, of course.

Preheat the grill to its highest setting. Place the chillies on the grill pan and toast them lightly under the grill for about 10 seconds – be careful they do not burn. Open up the chillies and return them to the grill to toast the insides. Place them in a blender with the garlic, spring onions, vinegar, orange juice, cumin seeds, herbs and water and blitz to a smooth purée.

Heat the vegetable oil in a saucepan, add the adobado mixture and the brown sugar and fry for 5–6 minutes, until the oil comes to the surface and the sauce has reduced. Transfer to a large bowl and leave to cool.

Meanwhile, prepare the ceviche. Discard the fronds and outer layers of the fennel, take off any stringy bits with a vegetable peeler and then cut each bulb in half vertically. Shred very thinly, preferably on a mandoline, and place in a bowl of iced water for about 20 minutes to curl up. Trim the radishes, shred them thinly and place in the iced water too.

Drain the fennel and radishes and place them in a bowl. Add the leaves from the coriander and toss together. Season with salt and pepper, then add the oil, lime juice and garlic and leave to marinate for 20 minutes.

Marinate the snapper fillets in the adobado mixture for 15 minutes, then grill for 3–4 minutes on each side under an overhead grill or on a ridged grill pan. Spoon over a little of the oil from the adobado. To serve, put the ceviche on individual serving plates and top with the grilled snapper.

1 chipotle chilli

1 ancho chilli

2 garlic cloves, chopped

2 spring onions, chopped

2 tablespoons red wine vinegar

3 tablespoons fresh orange juice

1/2 teaspoon cumin seeds

1 teaspoon dried oregano, preferably Mexican

1/2 teaspoon dried thyme

5 tablespoons water

6 tablespoons vegetable oil

2 tablespoons brown sugar

4 x 175g (6oz) snapper fillets

For the ceviche:

2 fennel bulbs

1 red oriental radish

1 green oriental radish

A bunch of fresh coriander

4 tablespoons olive oil

4 tablespoons lime juice

1 garlic clove, crushed

Salt and freshly ground black pepper

Sugar-seared tuna
with sticky rice cakes, choi sum and ginger–lime ponzu

Marinating fish in brown sugar or palm sugar is a favourite trick of mine as it gives it a beautifully caramelised exterior. Ponzu, a Japanese dipping sauce used for sashimi, sushi and other dishes, makes a good, tart contrast. It is very simple to prepare and wonderfully tasty. A word of advice would be to make a large amount of it, since you'll find yourself looking for more – it really is good! Try it with all manner of grilled seafood.

To make the marinade, gently heat the sugar in a pan until dissolved,then add 150ml (1/4 pint) of water and bring to the boil. Boil for 2 minutes, until sticky in consistency. Add the nam pla and chilli sauce and cook for 1 minute, then pour into a bowl. Stir in the garlic, ginger and lime juice and leave to cool. Place the tuna steaks in the marinade, turning to coat them, and leave for 2 hours.

In a bowl, combine the cooked rice with 4 of the spring onions and shape into 4 patties, about 7.5cm (3in) in diameter and 2cm (3/4in) high. Steam the choi sum and season with half the sesame oil and some salt and pepper. Keep warm.

Heat the vegetable oil in a large frying pan until almost smoking. Remove the tuna from the marinade, add to the pan and fry quickly for about 1 minute on each side, until browned and caramelised. Remove from the pan and keep warm.

Fry the spring onion cakes in the remaining sesame oil until golden and crisp.

For the ponzu, simply place all the ingredients in a pan and bring to boiling point, then remove from the heat.

To serve, arrange a spring onion cake on each serving plate, drape over the choi sum and top with the caramelised tuna. Sprinkle over the ponzu dressing and the remaining spring onions and serve immediately.

4 x 200g (7oz) tuna fillets
400g (14oz) cooked sushi rice
  (or other glutinous rice)
6 spring onions, finely shredded
350g (12oz) choi sum (Chinese
  flowering cabbage)
2 tablespoons sesame oil
4 tablespoons vegetable oil

For the marinade:
50g (2oz) brown sugar
1 tablespoon nam pla (Thai fish sauce)
1 tablespoon sweet chilli sauce
1 garlic clove, crushed
2.5cm (1in) piece of fresh root ginger,
  finely grated
Juice of 1/2 lime

For the ginger–lime ponzu:
Juice of 1 lime
2 tablespoons rice vinegar
4cm (11/2in) piece of fresh root ginger,
  finely chopped
2 tablespoons dark soy sauce
1 tablespoon mirin (Japanese sweet
  rice wine)
100ml (31/2fl oz) well-flavoured
  chicken stock
1 tablespoon chopped coriander

*Sri Lankan stir-fried squid
with garlic and ginger paste

Rice and stir-fried greens make good accompaniments to this simple dish.

Place the onion, garlic, ginger and chillies in a blender or food processor and blitz to a smooth paste. Heat 100ml (3 1/2 fl oz) of the olive oil in a pan, add the paste and cook over a low heat for 10–12 minutes, until aromatic and golden. Add the spice mix and cook for 5 minutes, then stir in the coconut milk and 150ml (1/4 pint) of water and bring to the boil. Reduce the heat and simmer for a further 10–15 minutes, until the sauce has thickened slightly.

Heat the remaining oil in a wok or large frying pan over a high heat. Add the squid and stir-fry for 1 minute to seal. Add the sauce and toss together for 1 minute, then serve.

1 onion, roughly chopped

2 garlic cloves, crushed

2.5cm (1in) piece of fresh root ginger, roughly chopped

2 red Thai chillies, chopped

150ml (1/4 pint) olive oil

2 tablespoons Sri Lankan spice mix (see p157)

150ml (1/4 pint) coconut milk

450g (1lb) cleaned young squid, tentacles left whole, body cut into rings

Seafood gumbo

Gumbo is a much-loved speciality of Louisiana, a great soup for those with big appetites, I think it makes a hearty main course too, which explains the large quantities in this recipe.

Scrub the mussels and clams under cold running water, removing the beards from the mussels and discarding any open mussels or clams that don't close when tapped on a work surface. Put them in a large pan, cover with the chicken stock and bring to the boil. Cook over a high heat for about 2–3 minutes, shaking the pan occasionally, until the mussels and clams open. Drain in a colander and strain the stock through a fine sieve. Shell the mussels and clams, discarding the shells.

Heat the oil in a heavy-based pan, then stir in the flour to make a roux. Stir constantly over a medi-um-high heat until it turns a deep brown (about the colour of peanut butter); this will take about 10–15 minutes. Add the onion, green pepper and celery, reduce the heat and cook gently for 5 minutes. Add the sausage, tomatoes and garlic, and whisk in the reserved stock a little at a time. Add the spring onions and bring to the boil, stirring frequently. Stir in the Worcestershire sauce and simmer for 40 minutes, skimming off the fat that rises to the top.

Add the mussels, clams, prawns and crabmeat to the soup and cook for 5 minutes. Season with salt and Tabasco to taste, then serve.

450g (1lb) mussels

450g (1lb) venus clams

1.5 litres (2 1/2 pints) well-flavoured chicken stock

4 tablespoons vegetable oil

50g (2oz) plain flour

1 onion, chopped

1 green pepper, chopped

1 celery stick, chopped

50g (2oz) andouille or chorizo sausage, sliced

225g (8oz) tomatoes, diced

1 garlic clove, crushed

6 spring onions, shredded

1 tablespoon Worcestershire sauce

450g (1lb) large raw tiger prawns, peeled and de-veined

100g (4oz) white crabmeat

Tabasco sauce

Salt

Cioppino
(seafood stew)

From the Italian community of San Francisco, this is similar to the classic fish stews of Italy, fired up with a little dried chilli. It's a great winter dish, best served with chunks of bread for dipping. Use any mixture of fish and shellfish you can lay your hands on.

Scrub the mussels and clams under cold running water, removing the beards from the mussels and discarding any open mussels or clams that don't close when tapped on a work surface.

Heat half the olive oil in a saucepan, add the garlic, shallots and fennel and cook gently until golden. Add the white wine and simmer until reduced by half. Add the tomato passata and both fish and chicken stocks. Bring to the boil, then add the herbs and chilli flakes and simmer over a low heat for 15 minutes.

Meanwhile, cut the snapper fillet into diamonds, then sauté in the remaining oil in a large pan until golden brown on both sides. Add the mussels, clams, prawns and squid. Pour over the tomato broth and raise the heat. Cover and cook until the clams and mussels open. Season to taste, then transfer to a large soup tureen and serve.

450g (1lb) mussels
450g (1lb) clams
4 tablespoons olive oil
1 garlic clove, crushed
2 shallots, chopped
1 fennel bulb, finely diced
100ml (3½fl oz) white wine
90ml (3fl oz) tomato passata
150ml (¼ pint) fish stock
150ml (¼ pint) chicken stock
1 tablespoon chopped mixed herbs, such as parsley, chervil and basil
½ teaspoon dried red chilli flakes
350g (12oz) red snapper fillet
12 large raw tiger prawns, peeled and de-veined
150g (5oz) small squid, cut into pieces
Salt and freshly ground black pepper

Tiger prawn, tomato and date curry

I picked up this recipe during a stint working in Singapore, where it is usually made with lobster. Traditionally the red dates unique to the area are used but it is just as good with ordinary dates.

Heat a large frying pan or a wok over a high heat, add half the oil, then season the prawns with a little salt and pepper and throw them into the pan. Stir-fry for 2–3 minutes, then remove from the pan and set aside.

Heat the remaining oil in the pan, add the green pepper and chillies and stir-fry for 1 minute. Stir in the curry paste and cook for 2 minutes or until fragrant. Add the coconut cream, the fish sauce, sugar, tomatoes and dates, reduce the heat and cook slowly for 5–8 minutes, stirring occasionally. Finally, return the prawns to the sauce and cook for a further minute.

Put the curry in a serving dish and sprinkle with the chopped coriander. Serve with fluffy, steamed white rice.

5 tablespoons vegetable oil
32 large raw tiger prawns, peeled and de-veined
1 green pepper, cut into 1cm (½in) dice
2 red Thai chillies, thinly sliced
3 tablespoons curry paste
350ml (12fl oz) unsweetened coconut cream
2 tablespoons nam pla (Thai fish sauce)
2 tablespoons caster sugar
450g (1lb) small tomatoes, skinned and chopped
12 fresh dates, stoned and cut in half
1 tablespoon chopped coriander
Salt and freshly ground black pepper

Prawns piri-piri

Piri-piri is the name of a hot chilli and also of this classic sauce, originally from Portuguese Africa. It can be searingly hot, so approach with caution.

Place the chillies, 150ml (1/4 pint) of the oil, the garlic and lemon juice in a blender and blitz to a purée. Heat the remaining oil in a large frying pan, season the prawns with a little salt and paprika and fry for 1–2 minutes until cooked. Add the jalapeño purée, blend together, and cook for 1 minute. Serve immediately, sprinkled with the parsley and accompanied by steamed rice.

HOT TIP Leave a little of the tail shell on the prawns for an attractive presentation.

8 red jalapeño chillies, deseeded and chopped

175ml (6fl oz) olive oil

2 garlic cloves, chopped

Juice of 1 lemon

24 large raw tiger prawns, peeled and de-veined

Smoked paprika

1 tablespoon chopped parsley

Salt

✳ Goan red masala lobster

I could live on this dish seven days a week. Like much of Goan cuisine, it is hot, sweet and fragrant. Scottish lobsters have the finest flavour, so do use these if you can find them. Basmati rice, plainly steamed or flavoured with turmeric, makes the best accompaniment.

First make the masala: toast the coriander and cumin seeds in a hot pan, then place them in a spice mill or coffee grinder and blitz to a fine powder. Put the coconut cream, turmeric, ginger, garlic and chilli powder in a blender with 150ml (1/4 pint) of water and purée until smooth. Add the ground seeds and set aside.

Heat the vegetable oil in a large frying pan, add the onion and cook until golden. Pour in the prepared masala and cook over a moderate heat until the liquid has evaporated and the oil has separated from the spice mixture. Cook for a further 10–15 minutes, then add another 150ml (1/4 pint) of water and simmer over a moderate heat until the mixture has reduced by about a quarter in volume. Add the tomatoes, tomato purée, garam masala and lobster.

Season to taste and cook for 3–4 minutes to heat through. Sprinkle with the chopped coriander and served accompanied by the lime wedges.

HOT TIP It is very easy to make your own garam masala. Just mix together 4 teaspoons of freshly ground cardamom and 1 teaspoon each of freshly ground cinnamon, cloves, cumin and black pepper. Store in an airtight container.

2 tablespoons vegetable oil

1 onion, finely chopped

4 plum tomatoes, skinned, deseeded and roughly chopped

2 teaspoons tomato purée

1/2 teaspoon garam masala (see Hot Tip)

4 x 675g (1 1/2 lb) cooked lobsters, preferably Scottish, cut into sections, claws cracked

2 tablespoons chopped coriander

1 lime, cut into wedges

Salt and freshly ground black pepper

For the masala:

2 teaspoons coriander seeds

2 teaspoons cumin seeds

1/2 packet of unsweetened coconut cream

1 teaspoon ground turmeric

5cm (2in) piece of fresh root ginger, chopped

4 garlic cloves, crushed

1/2 teaspoon chilli powder

poultry and meat

Guinea fowl
with smoked sausages, cannellini beans and mustard jus

Place the soaked cannellini beans in a pan, cover with plenty of cold water and bring to the boil. Simmer for 1 hour or until tender, then drain.

Preheat the oven to 200°C/400°F/gas mark 6. Season the guinea fowl breasts with salt and pepper. Heat the oil in a large frying pan, add the guinea fowl and cook, skin-side down, for 2–3 minutes, until golden. Remove from the pan and set aside.

Add the garlic, mushrooms, lardons and sausages to the pan and sauté over a low heat until coloured. Add the stock and cook for 10 minutes, then add the cannellini beans. Stir in the mustard and bay leaf, then transfer everything to a casserole dish. Top the beans with the guinea fowl, cover and place in the oven for 20–25 minutes, until the guinea fowl is cooked.

Serve straight from the oven, accompanied with creamy mashed potatoes.

175g (6oz) cannellini beans, soaked in
    water overnight and then drained
4 x 200g (7oz) guinea fowl breasts
4 tablespoons vegetable oil
1 garlic clove, crushed
75g (3oz) wild mushrooms, cut up if large
75g (3oz) piece of smoked bacon, cut
    into lardons
4 smoked pork sausages, skinned and
    cut into slices
300ml (1/2 pint) chicken stock
1 tablespoon tarragon mustard
1 bay leaf
Salt and freshly ground black pepper

Honey-roasted duck
with nutmeg and dried tangerine peel

I use nutmeg quite a lot in cooking. It has a subtle, scented heat. Cooking the duck in this way gives it a wonderful sweet, shiny glaze, similar to Peking duck. Serve with buttered Swiss chard, or with pak choi for a more authentic accompaniment.

Blanch the duck breasts in a large pan of boiling salted water for 2 minutes, then plunge them into a bowl of iced water. Remove and dry on a cloth.

In a blender, blitz together the honey or maple syrup, lime juice, olive oil, five-spice powder and nutmeg. Coat the duck breasts in this mixture, then sprinkle with the Szechuan pepper and sear in a heavy-based frying pan over a moderate heat until well done (alternatively cook in a moderate oven for 15–20 minutes). The duck should be cooked slowly and become glazed and caramel coloured.

Remove the duck from the pan and keep warm. Add the balsamic vinegar, chicken stock, *ketjap manis*, ginger, chilli, tangerine juice and chopped dried peel to the pan. Bring to the boil and simmer until reduced and syrupy in consistency.

Cut the duck into neat slices, coat with the sauce and serve.

HOT TIP Dried tangerine peel is available from oriental supermarkets and is also simple to prepare at home. Peel a tangerine and place the peel in a very low oven to dry for about 2 hours, until crisp. Chop finely and store in an airtight container.

4 x 225g (8oz) duck breasts
2 tablespoons honey or maple syrup
2 tablespoons lime juice
6 tablespoons olive oil
1 teaspoon five-spice powder
1/2 teaspoon grated nutmeg
1/2 teaspoon Szechuan pepper
1 tablespoon balsamic vinegar
600ml (1 pint) well-flavoured
    chicken stock
4 tablespoons ketjap manis
    (Indonesian soy sauce)
2.5cm (1in) piece of fresh root ginger,
    finely chopped
1 red Thai chilli, thinly sliced
Juice and dried peel of 2 tangerines
    (see Hot Tip)

Braised duck legs in tamarind sauce
with roasted jalapeño sweet potatoes

Blitz together all the marinade ingredients in a blender. Place the duck legs in a bowl, then spread over the blended spice mixture and leave to marinate for 2 hours.

Preheat the oven to 200°C/400°F/gas mark 6. Heat the oil in a heavy-based casserole. Remove the duck from the marinade and fry them in the hot oil until golden all over. Add the curry leaves and fenugreek seeds and fry for 1 minute. Add the marinade and 300ml (1/2 pint) of water and mix well to form a sauce. Bring to the boil, then reduce the heat, cover and transfer to the oven. Cook for 50–60 minutes or until the duck is tender.

Meanwhile, toss the sweet potatoes with the oil and green chilli, season with salt and pepper and roast in the oven for 25–30 minutes, until they are well caramelised.

Remove the duck casserole from the oven, stir in the red chilli and coriander and adjust the seasoning. To serve, divide the sweet potatoes between 4 serving plates, top with the braised duck legs and pour over the sauce.

HOT TIP Tamarind is the pulp from the long, brown pods of the tamarind tree and has an intensely sour flavour. The most convenient form to buy it in is a paste – available from Asian shops, large supermarkets and some wholefood stores. But you can also buy blocks of compressed tamarind pods that have to be soaked in hot water and then squeezed out to extract the pulp.

4 large duck legs

4 tablespoons vegetable oil

6 curry leaves

1 teaspoon fenugreek seeds

1 red jalapeño chilli, deseeded and chopped

3 tablespoons chopped coriander

Salt and freshly ground black pepper

For the marinade:

1 tablespoon tamarind paste

1 red jalapeño chilli, chopped

1 tablespoon tomato purée

1 teaspoon salt

1 tablespoon sugar

2.5cm (1in) piece of fresh root ginger, chopped

1 garlic clove, chopped

1/2 teaspoon ground cumin

1 teaspoon coriander seeds

For the sweet potatoes:

450g (1lb) orange-fleshed sweet potatoes, peeled and cut into 2cm (3/4in) dice

4 tablespoons olive oil

1 green jalapeño chilli, thinly sliced

* 'Hot Morocco' chicken
with sweet spices and harissa

For the marinade, place all the ingredients in a blender and blitz to a smooth purée. Season the chicken pieces with a little salt and place them in a dish. Pour over the marinade and mix well, then leave to marinate for about 2 hours. Remove the chicken from the marinade.

Heat the olive oil in a frying pan and fry the chicken breasts for 6–8 minutes, until golden, turning once. Mix the tomato purée with the chicken stock. Pour the marinade over the chicken, add the stock and bring to the boil. Reduce the heat, then cover and cook for 8–10 minutes, until the sauce has reduced enough to coat the chicken. Serve sprinkled with the coriander.

3 tablespoons olive oil

Juice of 1 lemon

2 garlic cloves, crushed

1/2 teaspoon whole aniseed

1/2 teaspoon ground cinnamon

1/2 teaspoon ground ginger

1 teaspoon ground cumin

1 teaspoon ground coriander

1/2 teaspoon paprika

1 red jalapeño chilli, deseeded and diced

11/2 teaspoons Harissa (see p156)

For the chicken:

3 tablespoons olive oil

2 tablespoons coriander leaves

1 tablespoon tomato purée

600ml (1 pint) chicken stock

4 chicken breasts, boned and skinned

Salt

Sauté chicken Colombo

Serve this simple sauté with some fluffy white rice. I also like to have some fruit with it, such as pineapple, raisins and mango. Serving fruit with spicy dishes is typical of Caribbean cookery. If you cannot find a Habenero chilli, subsitute 1/2 teaspoon of West Indian hot pepper sauce.

Season the chicken pieces with salt, pepper and 1 tablespoon of the spice mix and leave for 2 hours.
Heat the oil in a heavy-based saucepan, add the chicken and sauté until lightly golden in colour; do not colour too much. Pour off the excess fat, add the onion and garlic and cook for 2 minutes. Stir in the remaining spice mix and cook over a low heat for 2 minutes. Add the remaining vegetables, plus the chilli and enough water just to cover the chicken. Bring to the boil, add the bay leaf, then reduce the heat, cover and cook for 30–40 minutes, until the chicken is tender.
Stir in the lime juice, check the seasoning and then serve immediately.

1 x 1.3kg (3lb) chicken, cut into 8 pieces

3 tablespoons Colombo spice mix
  (see p156) or mild curry powder

3 tablespoons vegetable oil

1 onion, chopped

3 garlic cloves, thinly sliced

4 spring onions, shredded

1 large aubergine, cut into 2cm
  (3/4in) dice

2 courgettes, cut into 2cm (3/4in) dice

1 habanero chilli, deseeded and chopped

1 bay leaf

3 tablespoons lime juice

Salt and freshly ground black pepper

A simple Mediterranean spice-roasted chicken

Preheat the oven to 200°C/400°F/gas mark 6. In a large bowl, mix together the coriander, parsley, cumin seeds, paprika, turmeric and some salt and pepper. Whisk in the oil, lemon juice and harissa. Generously coat the chicken with the spice mixture and leave to marinate for 2 hours.

Roast in the oven for 1–1¼ hours (see Hot Tip for stuffing suggestion), until the chicken is golden all over and the juices run clear when a skewer is inserted near the thigh bone.

Leave to rest for 15 minutes before carving and serving. This dish is equally delicious served cold.

HOT TIP This is nice filled with a fruity couscous stuffing before roasting. Simply cook couscous in some stock to which a little saffron has been added, then mix in some chopped no-need-to-soak dried figs, prunes and apricots, chopped coriander leaves and season to taste.

3 tablespoons chopped coriander
3 tablespoons chopped flat-leaf parsley
1 tablespoon cumin seeds
1½ teaspoons smoked paprika
1 teaspoon ground turmeric
150ml (¼ pint) olive oil
Juice of ½ lemon
2 tablespoons Harissa (see p156)
1 x 1.5kg (3½lb) roasting chicken
Salt and freshly ground black pepper

✳ Fiery Keralan chicken

A hot southern Indian dish for real chilli aficionados, flavoured with fragrant spices.

Heat half of the ghee or oil in a frying pan, add the onion and cook over a gentle heat until golden. Put the onion in a blender or food processor with the ginger, garlic, cumin, coriander, fenugreek, peppercorns, vinegar and ½ teaspoon of salt. Process until smooth, then transfer to a bowl and add the turmeric, sugar, curry leaves, cardamom pods, cinnamon, aniseed and whole chillies.

Heat the remaining ghee or oil in a large heavy pan. Add the chicken pieces and fry for 10–12 minutes, until golden. Add the spice paste and raise the heat to seal the paste to the chicken. Add the tomato purée and the water or stock. Bring to the boil, reduce the heat and simmer until the chicken is very tender, adding a little more water if necessary. Season to taste and then serve with rice.

4 tablespoons ghee or vegetable oil
1 large onion, chopped
2.5cm (1in) piece of fresh root ginger, chopped
4 garlic cloves, chopped
2 teaspoons cumin seeds
2 teaspoons coriander seeds
2 teaspoons fenugreek seeds
2 teaspoons black peppercorns
4 tablespoons white wine vinegar
1 teaspoon ground turmeric
2 teaspoons caster sugar
4 curry leaves
10 fresh cardamom pods, cracked
1 teaspoon ground cinnamon
1 teaspoon whole aniseed
6 small De Arbol chillies
900g (2lb) chicken pieces, skinned
2 tablespoons tomato purée
300ml (½ pint) water or chicken stock
Salt and freshly ground black pepper

SIMPLE MEDITERRANEAN SPICE-ROASTED CHICKEN

Pollo verde
(chicken in Mexican-style green sauce)

This is an adaptation of a recipe from my good friend, Alicia De'Angeli, of the El Tajin restaurant in Mexico City, who visited the Lanesborough for a promotion on Mexican food. It is very good served with spinach and chargrilled corn.

Roast, peel and deseed the poblano chillies (see page 8–9), then chop them finely and set aside.
Place the chicken breasts in a single layer in a large saucepan or casserole. Bring the stock to the boil and pour it over the chicken, then cook on a low simmer for 5–8 minutes. Remove the chicken breasts from the pan and reserve the stock.

Place the chillies, onion, herbs, sesame seeds, peanuts, tomatillos, tortillas and lettuce leaves in a blender or food processor and purée until smooth. Heat the oil in a pan and add purée. Cook for 5 minutes and then stir in the reserved chicken stock. Season with salt, add the chicken to the sauce and simmer for 5 minutes, basting with the sauce.

HOT TIP Tomatillos are an indispensable part of Mexican cooking. They look like pale green tomatoes with a papery, lantern-shaped husk. Unripe tomatoes can be used instead, although they lack the tart, citrussy flavour of tomatillos. Canned tomatillos are available from large delicatessens, while some specialist shops stock fresh ones occasionally.

2 green poblano chillies
4 chicken breasts, skinned
900ml (1¼ pints) well-flavoured
*   chicken stock*
1 onion, chopped
50g (2oz) coriander leaves
50g (2oz) flat-leaf parsley
25g (1oz) sesame seeds, toasted in a
*   dry frying pan*
1 tablespoon roasted peanuts
150g (5oz) canned tomatillos (or
*   green tomatoes)*
2 corn tortillas, chopped
8 romaine (Cos) lettuce leaves, blanched
*   in boiling water and then refreshed*
2 tablespoons vegetable oil
Salt

Foil-steamed baby chicken
in fragrant wasabi soy broth

A dish to keep dieters happy, since there is no added fat. It tastes clean and refreshing, and cooking the chicken in foil parcels means that all the flavours are retained. I like to serve it with a little lemon and some fluffy white rice.

Preheat the oven to 200°C/400°F/gas mark 6. Cut each chicken in half down the centre. Season with a little salt, place in a dish, pour over half the sake and set aside.

Cut two 30cm (12in) squares of kitchen foil and place 2 chicken halves on each piece. Put the vegetables on top of the chicken and bring up the edges of the foil carefully around the chicken.

Bring the chicken stock to the boil with the soy sauce, the remaining sake and the lemon juice, then add the wasabi and remove from the heat.

Drizzle the flavoured stock over the chicken and twist the edges of the foil together to make a close seal. Place both parcels on a baking tray and place in the oven to steam for 20–25 minutes or until the chicken is cooked.

To serve, open the parcels at the table to release the wonderful aroma.

2 x 500g (18oz) poussins, spatchcocked
  (see Hot Tip)
4 tablespoons sake (or dry sherry)
1 carrot, cut into thin strips
4 spring onions, shredded
12 shiitake mushrooms, thinly sliced
150ml (1/4 pint) chicken stock
6 tablespoons light soy sauce
1 tablespoon lemon juice
1/2 teaspoon wasabi paste
Salt ·

HOT TIP To spatchcock a bird, cut out the backbone with kitchen scissors or poultry shears. Break the wishbone, then turn the bird cut-side down and flatten it by pressing down with the heel of your hand. Turn it over and remove all the ribcage bones. An easier option is to buy the poussins ready-spatchcocked from a supermarket or good butcher's!

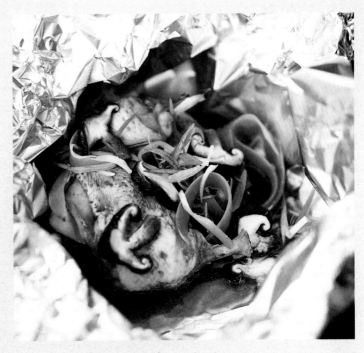

Braised chicken
with spiced lentils and peanut butter

Season the chicken liberally with salt and pepper. Heat the oil in a large, deep frying pan, add the chicken pieces and cook until golden all over. Add the garlic, onion and spices and mix with the chicken. Reduce the heat and cook until the spices become fragrant. Add the lentils, carrots and chicken stock and bring to the boil, then stir in the berbere. Reduce the heat and simmer for 40–45 minutes, until the chicken and lentils are tender, skimming off any fat that rises to the surface.

Stir in the peanut butter, adjust the seasoning and serve immediately.

1 x 1.5kg (3½lb) chicken, cut into 8

3 tablespoons vegetable or groundnut oil

1 garlic clove, crushed

1 onion, cut into 5mm (¼in) dice

¼ teaspoon cayenne pepper

½ teaspoon ground cinnamon

½ teaspoon ground cloves

½ teaspoon fennel seeds

150g (5oz) Puy lentils

2 carrots, sliced

600ml (1 pint) chicken stock

2 teaspoons Ethiopian Berbere
  (see p154)

4 tablespoons smooth peanut butter

Salt and freshly ground black pepper

Chocolate chilli glazed pork

There have been many doubters about this recipe but I've won over a fair few of them, including food writer Sophie Grigson. Do give it a try. The flavours are fantastic, and not as outlandish as they at first appear.

Chocolate and chilli are used a lot in Mexican cooking, resulting in a wonderful combination of sweetness and spice. I like to serve this with a fruity orange, red onion and cucumber salad.

Preheat the oven to 190°C/375°F/gas mark 5. Place the whole garlic cloves in a small baking tin, pour over a little oil and roast for 10–15 minutes, until soft and slightly charred. Leave to cool a little, then squeeze out the flesh.

Remove the stems and seeds from the ancho chillies. Soak the chillies in boiling water for 30 minutes, then drain. Place the chillies, achiote seeds and roasted garlic flesh in a blender with the herbs, vinegar, onion and spices. Add enough water to blend to a smooth purée, then add the sugar and a little salt and pepper.

Trim the pork belly and smear the chilli purée over it. Cover and refrigerate for at least 6–8 hours, preferably overnight.

Preheat the oven to 180°C/350°F/gas mark 4. Remove the pork from the refrigerator and wipe off the excess chilli purée. Place the pork in a baking tin, pour 100ml (3½fl oz) of water around it and cover with foil. Bake for 40–50 minutes, basting occasionally with the liquid. Remove the pork from the oven and cool slightly, discard the pan juices.

Blitz together all the ingredients for the glaze. Raise the oven heat to full, cut the pork into slices 5mm (¼in) thick, brush with the glaze and return to the oven for about 10–12 minutes.

4 garlic cloves

A little oil

4 ancho chillies

1½ teaspoons achiote seeds

1 tablespoon coriander leaves

1½ teaspoons fresh oregano

1 small bay leaf

100ml (3½fl oz) white wine vinegar

½ small onion, chopped

A pinch each of ground cumin, cloves
  and cinnamon

1 teaspoon sugar

750g (1lb 10oz) pork belly

Salt and freshly ground black pepper

For the glaze:

1 tablespoon clear honey, warmed

1 red chilli, deseeded and finely chopped

25g (1oz) bitter chocolate, melted

CHOCOLATE CHILLI GLAZED PORK

Chimichurri pork fillet

Chimichurri is a sort of Argentinian pesto, made with vinegar, oregano, garlic and oil. It works well with any grilled fish or meat and is also very good in a sandwich of grilled vegetables, Traditionally it doesn't contain any chilli but I prefer to include some. Be sure to use good-quality olive oil. Serve this dish with mashed potatoes and black beans.

Season the pork fillet with salt and pepper. Mix 4 tablespoons of the oil with the garlic and chilli powder, rub this mixture all over the pork fillet and leave to marinate for 1 hour.

To make the chimichurri sauce, put all the ingredients in a blender and blitz to a coarse purée.

Heat the remaining oil in a frying pan, add the pork fillets and fry for 3–4 minutes, turning them to give a wonderful golden colour all over. Leave to rest for a while and then cut into thick slices.

Place on a serving dish, pour over the chimichurri sauce and serve.

4 x 200g (7oz) pieces of pork fillet

6 tablespoons olive oil

1 garlic clove, crushed

1 tablespoon chilli powder

Salt and freshly ground black pepper

For the chimichurri sauce:

3 garlic cloves, crushed

A small bunch of coriander

A small bunch of flat-leaf parsley

*1 tablespoon fresh oregano (or
 1 teaspoon dried)*

*1 jalapeño chilli, deseeded and roughly
 chopped*

150ml (1/4 pint) olive oil

4 tablespoons white wine vinegar

Braised pork belly
with Chinese spicy bean sauce

Preheat the oven to 190°C/375°F/gas mark 5. Season the pork liberally with the five-spice powder and some salt and pepper. Heat the oil in a casserole, add the pork and seal it well all over, then remove and set aside. Add the lemongrass, ginger, garlic, onion and rice vinegar to the casserole and bring to the boil. Then add the plum sauce, black bean sauce, star anise, soy sauce and chicken stock and return to the boil.

Return the pork to the sauce, cover the casserole with a lid and place in the oven to braise for 1–11/2 hours. Remove the pork from the sauce and keep warm. Strain the sauce and keep warm.

For the garnish, heat the sesame oil in a wok or large frying pan, add the pak choi, garlic and ginger and stir-fry for 1 minute. Place in a serving dish. Slice the pork and place it on the pak choi. Pour over the sauce and serve.

750g (1lb 10oz) pork belly

2 tablespoons five-spice powder

4 tablespoons vegetable oil

3 lemongrass stalks, outer layers removed, chopped

5cm (2in) piece of fresh ginger, chopped

1 garlic clove, crushed

1 onion, thinly sliced

150ml (1/4 pint) rice vinegar

300ml (1/2 pint) plum sauce

2 tablespoons Chinese spicy bean sauce

2 star anise

2 tablespoons soy sauce

3 tablespoons chicken stock

Salt and freshly ground black pepper

For the garnish:

4 tablespoons sesame oil

500g (18oz) pak choi

1 teaspoon crushed garlic

2.5cm (2in) piece of fresh ginger, chopped

Barbecue oregano-cured pork rack

I like to serve this with steamed spring greens tossed with garlic and olive oil.

Place the chillies, onion and garlic in a blender or food processor and blitz to a purée. Add the chilli powder, cumin, oregano, sugar and vinegar and blend well. Rub the mixture into the pork rack and leave to marinate overnight.

The next day, rub the olive oil over the pork rack.

Place the pork rack on a barbecue and cook for about 5 minutes on each side to seal all over, then move it to the edge of the grill (or raise the grill rack) to allow it to cook slowly for about 15–20 minutes. Leave the meat to rest for 10 minutes before serving.

HOT TIP If your butcher hasn't French trimmed the pork rack, here's how to do it: remove the skin, then cut away the layer of meat and fat from the top 5cm (2in) of the bones. Clean the bones by scraping off all the remaining bits of flesh.

8-bone pork rack, French trimmed (see Hot Tip)

2 red serrano chillies, chopped

1 onion, chopped

4 garlic cloves, crushed

1 tablespoon chilli powder

1 teaspoon ground cumin

2 teaspoons fresh oregano

2 tablespoons sugar

1 tablespoon white wine vinegar or cider vinegar

4 tablespoons olive oil

Braised lamb's kidneys
with chorizo, bacon, broad beans and grain mustard polenta

For the polenta, put the milk and oil in a heavy-based pan and bring to the boil. Reduce to a simmer and then gradually rain in the polenta, stirring constantly. Reduce the heat and cook, stirring, for 15 minutes or until the polenta leaves the side of the pan. Stir in the Parmesan, butter and cream, then the mustard. Season with salt and pepper and keep warm.

Peel the outer membrane off each kidney, cut them in half and remove the central core. Heat the oil in a large frying pan, season the kidneys and fry them in the hot oil for 3–4 minutes, until lightly coloured. Remove from the pan and keep warm. Add the bacon lardons and chorizo to the pan and fry until lightly coloured, then remove and set aside. Stir in the sherry and stock and simmer for 10 minutes, until the sauce reduces and thickens. Add the tarragon and whisk in the butter. Return all the meat to the sauce, together with the broad beans, and adjust the seasoning.

Put the mustard polenta on serving plates and top with the kidney mixture. Serve immediately.

12 lamb's kidneys

4 tablespoons vegetable oil

50g (2oz) piece of streaky bacon, cut into lardons

150g (5oz) chorizo sliced 1cm (1/2in) thick

100ml (31/2fl oz) sherry

600ml (1 pint) meat stock

10 tarragon leaves

15g (1/2oz) unsalted butter

50g (2oz) broad beans, blanched

Salt and freshly ground black pepper

For the grain mustard polenta:

600ml (1 pint) milk

3 tablespoons olive oil

250g (9oz) polenta

150g (5oz) Parmesan, finely grated

100g (4oz) unsalted butter

100ml (31/2fl oz) double cream

2 tablespoons grain mustard

Red-cooked chargrilled lamb

A dish inspired by the cooking of Mexico's Yucatan peninsula, this uses a bright, richly flavoured marinade based on the Hot achiote baste on page 146. It is very simple to prepare and ideal for a summer barbecue.

Put the chillies, garlic, onion and achiote baste in a blender or food processor and blitz until smooth. Then add all the remaining ingredients except the lamb and blitz again to make a marinade. Pour into a deep dish, immerse the lamb steaks in the marinade and leave for 1–2 hours.

Remove the lamb from the dish and brush off any excess marinade. Place on a barbecue or ridged grill pan and cook for between 5 and 8 minutes on each side, until nicely chargrilled. Serve immediately with a Hot Mexican salsa (see page 151), if liked.

4 red jalapeño chillies, chopped

2 garlic cloves, chopped

1 small onion, chopped

1 tablespoon Hot achiote baste (see p146)

150ml (1/4 pint) fresh orange juice

100ml (31/2fl oz) tomato ketchup

1 teaspoon dried oregano

2 teaspoons Dijon mustard

2 tablespoons Worcestershire sauce

4 tablespoons white wine vinegar

4 lamb leg steaks, cut horizontally from the leg, weighing 225–300g (8–10oz) each

Lamb sosaties
with tsire

Sosaties are South African kebabs, prepared with all manner of meats. Their roots probably lie in Malaysian cuisine, since the name derives from the Malay word *sate*, or spiced sauce. Tsire is also South African, a mixture of ground peanuts, chilli and spices that is usually sprinkled over chargrilled meat. These sosaties are excellent served with couscous or tabbouleh.

Pat the lamb dry and place in a large bowl. Add the grated onion, garlic, ginger, coriander, curry powder, apricot jam, turmeric and some salt and pepper. Scatter over the chilli and lemon zest, then pour over the vinegar and mix well. Cover with clingfilm and chill for up to 6 hours.

Remove the meat from the marinade and thread on to 4 large skewers. Sprinkle over the chopped bay leaves and grill or barbecue the skewers for 8–10 minutes, turning occasionally, until cooked.

Meanwhile, put the peanuts in a blender or food processor and blitz coarsely. Add the mixed spice, chilli powder and some salt and blitz for 3 seconds, keeping the mixture like small niblets.

When the sosaties are cooked, transfer to a serving dish and scatter the tsire on top.

450g (1lb) lamb (leg or shoulder), cut into 2.5cm (1in) cubes
1 onion, grated
2 garlic cloves, crushed
2 teaspoons ground ginger
2 teaspoons ground coriander
1 tablespoon curry powder
4 teaspoons apricot jam
1 teaspoon ground turmeric
1 serrano chilli, deseeded and finely chopped
1 teaspoon grated lemon zest
1 tablespoon white wine vinegar
2 bay leaves, finely chopped
Salt and freshly ground black pepper

For the tsire:
50g (2oz) salted peanuts
1 teaspoon ground mixed spice
1 teaspoon chilli powder
Salt

Slow-cooked lamb shanks
with tchermila and spiced aubergines

Lamb shanks are given a Middle Eastern treatment in this dish, with a fragrant tchermila spice paste. As the name implies, this is very similar to the Moroccan chermoula. The paste can be kept in the fridge in an airtight container for 2 weeks or in the freezer for 1 month.

Place all the ingredients for the tchermila paste in a blender and blitz until smooth. Season the lamb shanks with salt, then rub them all over with the paste. Cover and leave to marinate for at least 2 hours, preferably 8 hours.

Preheat the oven to 150°C/300°F/gas mark 2. Heat 3 tablespoons of the oil in a large casserole over a high heat. Add the shanks and brown them all over for 5–8 minutes, then remove from the casserole. Add the remaining oil to the casserole, then throw in the onion, reduce the heat and cook for 1 minute. Add the ginger, cinnamon and tomatoes and cook briefly to meld the flavours. Return the lamb shanks to the casserole and stir to mix with the spices and tomatoes. Pour over the orange juice and stock or water, season with salt and pepper and bring to the boil. Cover the casserole, transfer to the oven and cook for about 2 hours, basting the meat regularly.

Cut the aubergines in half lengthways, then cut across into slices 2cm (3/4in) thick. Heat the olive oil in a large frying pan, toss the aubergines with the garlic and ground cumin and fry in the hot oil for 2 minutes, until sealed and golden on both sides. Remove the lid from the lamb, tuck in the aubergines, then cover again and bake for another 30 minutes. The lamb should be very tender, with little sauce remaining.

Serve with Israeli couscous, either plain or flavoured with saffron.

HOT TIP If you prefer, you can replace the spiced aubergines with root vegetables such as turnips, parsnips and carrots. Lightly seal them in the pan after frying the onion and then braise in the oven with the lamb.

4 x 450–500g (16–18oz) lamb shanks
4 tablespoons vegetable oil
1 onion, finely chopped
1cm (1/2in) piece of fresh root ginger,
  finely chopped
1 teaspoon ground cinnamon
400g (14oz) can of tomatoes, chopped
150ml (1/4 pint) fresh orange juice
300ml (1/2 pint) meat stock or water
Salt and freshly ground black pepper

For the tchermila paste:

1 teaspoon saffron strands
3 garlic cloves, crushed
1 teaspoon coriander seeds
1 teaspoon cumin seeds
1 serrano chilli, deseeded
1 onion, finely grated
1 tablespoon Harissa, (see p156)
1 teaspoon hot paprika
4 tablespoons olive oil

For the spiced aubergines:

2 large aubergines
100ml (31/2fl oz) olive oil
2 garlic cloves, crushed
1 teaspoon ground cumin

Asian-style steak au poivre

This take on the classic French peppered steak is inspired by my love of oriental food. The vegetables should remain crisp, the steak peppery, with a slightly sweet sauce.

Mix the cracked peppercorns together and then, using the heel of your hand, press them evenly over one side of each steak. Leave for 30 minutes.

Heat the oil in a large, heavy-based frying pan until smoking. Season the steaks with salt, then add them to the pan, pepper-side down. Fry over a moderate heat, turning once, for 3–4 minutes for medium-rare, longer if you prefer your meat more cooked. Remove from the pan and keep warm.

Spoon off any fat from the pan, then return it to the heat, add the cognac and flambé it with a match, standing well back. When the flames have died down, add the mirin, corn syrup or honey, ginger, chicken stock and soy sauces. Bring to the boil, then reduce the heat and simmer until the liquid is reduced by half its volume. Stir in the arrowroot mixture and boil for 1 minute, until thickened, then strain through a fine sieve into a clean pan. Finally whisk in the butter a piece at a time. Keep warm while you prepare the vegetables.

For the vegetables, heat the sesame oil in a wok or large frying pan, add the garlic and ginger and leave to infuse for 10 seconds. Add the vegetables, stir-fry for 3–4 minutes, then season. Arrange on 4 serving plates, place the fillet steak on top and pour the sauce over.

HOT TIP This recipe is also very good made with a meaty fish such as monkfish or turbot.

1 tablespoon black peppercorns, coarsely cracked (see Hot Tip on p28)

1 tablespoon Szechuan peppercorns, cracked (see Hot Tip on p28)

4 x 175g (6oz) fillet steaks

4 tablespoons vegetable oil

2 tablespoons cognac

4 tablespoons mirin (Japanese sweet rice wine)

1 tablespoon corn syrup or honey

2.5cm (1in) piece of fresh root ginger, grated

600ml (1 pint) well-flavoured chicken stock

4 tablespoons light soy sauce

1 tablespoon ketjap manis (Indonesian soy sauce)

2 teaspoons arrowroot, mixed with 2 teaspoons cold water

25g (1oz) unsalted butter, diced

Salt

For the vegetables:

3 tablespoons sesame oil

1 garlic clove, crushed

1cm (1/2in) piece of fresh root ginger, thinly shredded

4 small pak choi, separated into leaves

1 carrot, sliced

8 spring onions, halved

100g (4oz) shiitake mushrooms, thickly sliced

2 red radishes, sliced

50g (2oz) beansprouts

Seared calf's liver
with chorizo lentils and purple mash

Spicy sausage and lentils are a perfect marriage and I often combine them in a soup. Here they make a hearty accompaniment for seared calf's liver. This dish featured on the menu at the Lanesborough for a while and was very popular.

Pick over the lentils and wash them 3 times in clean water. Put them in a pan, cover with cold water, then bring to the boil and simmer for 30–40 minutes, until tender. Stir from time to time and add more water if the lentils become too dry. When they are cooked they should be moist but not soupy in consistency.

Heat 1 tablespoon of the oil in a frying pan, add the onion, carrot, chilli and spices and cook for 1 minute. Add the chorizo slices, toss together and cook for a further minute, then add to the lentils. Stir in the coriander and butter, adjust the seasoning and keep warm.

Preheat the oven to 190°C/375°F/gas mark 5. Place the whole garlic cloves in a small baking tin, pour over the olive oil and roast for 10–15 minutes, until tender. Remove from the oven and keep warm.

Meanwhile, cook the whole potatoes in a pan of boiling salted water until tender, then drain and peel (peeling them after cooking preserves their wonderful colour). Mash to a smooth purée, return to the heat and stir in the oil, butter and cream. Season to taste. The purée should be really smooth and silky in texture.

Heat the remaining oil in a frying pan until very hot. Season the liver with salt and pepper and cook for 1 minute on each side, keeping it pink inside.

To serve, put a bed of the spiced lentils on individual serving plates and top with 2 slices of liver. Garnish with the roasted garlic cloves and put a mound of purple mash on the side.

150g (5oz) Puy lentils

3 tablespoons vegetable oil

1 onion, chopped

1 carrot, finely diced

1 red chilli, deseeded and finely diced

1/2 teaspoon ground cumin

1/2 teaspoon ground coriander

125g (41/2oz) chorizo sausage, sliced into rounds 1cm (1/2in) thick

1 tablespoon chopped coriander

25g (1oz) butter

12 garlic cloves

2 tablespoons olive oil

8 x 75g (3oz) thick slices of calf's liver

Salt and freshly ground black pepper

For the purple mash:

450g (1lb) truffle potatoes (sometimes labelled as purple or black potatoes)

2 tablespoons olive oil

75g (3oz) unsalted butter

100ml (31/2fl oz) double cream

Venison chilli
with dried fruit, oregano and crumbled goat's cheese

If you can get hold of Mexican oregano for this chilli, do use it. It has a more pungent flavour and grassy aroma than the European variety.

Preheat the oven to 180°C/350°F/gas mark 4. Remove the stems and seeds from the chipotle chillies and roast the chillies in the oven for 1–2 minutes. Place them in a pan, cover with water, then bring to the boil and simmer for 30 minutes. Drain the chillies and place them in a blender. Blitz with enough of their cooking water to make a paste.

Heat the vegetable oil in a large, heavy-based casserole. Season the venison with a little salt and then fry in batches in the hot oil until sealed and golden brown on all sides, transferring to a plate as each batch is done. Add the onion, garlic, bay leaf, coriander and cumin and cook until the onion is soft and translucent. Return the meat to the pan, then add the chipotle chilli paste, chilli powder and tomato purée and cook for 10 minutes to amalgamate the flavours. Pour in the beer and stock, add the brown sugar and cook for 5 minutes, then mix together well, season with salt and pepper and bring to the boil. Reduce the heat to a simmer and add the dried fruit and oregano. Cover and transfer to the preheated oven to cook for 11/4 hours, stirring occasionally. Add the cooked beans and cook for a further 20 minutes.

To serve, put the chilli in a large soup tureen and sprinkle over the crumbled goat's cheese and the corn tortilla chips, if using.

HOT TIP This dish freezes well. Cook for 11/4 hours, then add the beans and leave to cool. Place in an airtight container and freeze for up to 1 month. For best results, reheat from frozen.

3 chipotle chillies

4 tablespoons vegetable oil

675g (11/2lb) venison (shoulder or leg), cut into 2cm (3/4in) dice

1 onion, chopped

2 garlic cloves, crushed

1 bay leaf

1 teaspoon ground coriander

1/2 teaspoon ground cumin

1 tablespoon chilli powder

2 tablespoons tomato purée

150ml (1/4 pint) brown ale

1 litre (13/4 pints) meat stock

2 tablespoons brown sugar

50g (2oz) no-need-to-soak dried apricots, cut in half

75g (3oz) no-need-to-soak dried prunes, cut in half

1 tablespoon dried oregano, preferably Mexican

175g (6oz) cooked black beans (or kidney beans)

150g (5oz) mature goat's cheese, crumbled

Corn tortilla chips, to garnish (optional)

Salt and freshly ground black pepper

vegetables

Sweet and sour baby onions
with chilli and raisin jam

This makes a great accompaniment to grilled chicken or pork. Serve as a relish or as a vegetable side dish, in which case you may want to double the quantities.

Preheat the oven to 200°C/400°F/gas mark 6. Place the onions in a small roasting tin in a single layer and pour over the oil. Toss, season lightly and place in the oven to roast for 12–15 minutes.

Remove from the oven, add the vinegar, stock and chilli jam and stir to combine. Return to the oven for 10 minutes. Place in a serving dish and coat with any remaining cooking juices.

350g (12oz) baby button onions, peeled
4 tablespoons vegetable oil
2 tablespoons balsamic vinegar
150ml (1/4 pint) chicken stock
2 tablespoons Chilli and raisin jam
  (see p148)
Salt and freshly ground black pepper

Chargrilled baby aubergines
with ginger pesto

Pesto is such a versatile ingredient that it has become a kitchen basic in recent years. Aubergine and ginger were made for each other, so here's an oriental variation on a theme.

To make the pesto, process all the ingredients together in a blender or food processor, adding enough oil to form a paste.

Cut the aubergines in half lengthways, brush with half the olive oil and place under a hot grill, cut-side down, for 4–5 minutes or until the skins blister and become slightly charred. Turn the aubergines over, brush with the remaining oil and grill for 5 minutes, until soft and tender. Serve topped with a dollop of ginger pesto.

8 baby aubergines, 7.5–10cm
(3–4in) long
6 tablespoons olive oil
For the ginger pesto:
2 tablespoons basil leaves
2 tablespoons mint leaves
2 garlic cloves, crushed
25g (1oz) roasted peanuts
5cm (2in) piece of fresh root ginger,
finely chopped
A pinch of sugar
About 2 tablespoons vegetable oil
Salt

Stuffed cherry chilli peppers
with olives and Gruyère

Preheat the oven to 200°C/400°F/gas mark 6. Slice the top off the peppers and remove the seeds. Melt half the butter in a frying pan, add the onion and garlic and cook for 5 minutes, until softened. Remove from the heat and stir in the pine kernels, olives, herbs, mustard, breadcrumbs and two thirds of the cheese. Divide the stuffing between the chilli peppers and place them in a baking dish.

Heat the remaining butter in a small pan, stir in the flour and cook gently for 1–2 minutes. Gradually stir in the milk, then bring to the boil and simmer for a few minutes, until the sauce thickens. Season to taste and stir in the remaining cheese. Pour the sauce over the peppers, cover with foil and bake for 10–15 minutes. Remove the foil and cook for 10–15 minutes longer, until the topping is golden, then serve immediately.

HOT TIP If you cannot find Hungarian cherry chilli peppers they can be replaced with small poblano chillies or even baby red peppers.

6 small to medium Hungarian
cherry chilli peppers
50g (2oz) unsalted butter
1 red onion, finely chopped
2 garlic cloves, crushed
50g (2oz) pine kernels, toasted
100g (4oz) black olives, chopped
3 tablespoons chopped mixed herbs
(such as basil, oregano and rosemary)
2 teaspoons Dijon mustard
100g (4oz) fresh white breadcrumbs
150g (5oz) Gruyère cheese, finely grated
25g (1oz) plain flour
300ml (1/2 pint) full-fat milk
Salt and freshly ground black pepper

Szechuan hot fried vegetables
with spicy bean sauce

You could try other combinations of vegetables here, as long as you choose contrasting colours and textures. The heat comes from Chinese black bean sauce – an easy way of spicing up stir-fries and other oriental dishes.

Heat the oil in a wok or a large frying pan, add the garlic and ginger and leave to infuse for 30 seconds. Add the vegetables and water chestnuts and stir-fry for about 3–4 minutes, until crisp and tender. Add the *ketjap manis* and cornflour paste and stir-fry until the vegetables are glazed in the soy sauce. Add the black bean sauce and 150ml (1/4 pint) of water and bring to the boil, then season to taste. Transfer to a serving bowl, scatter on the cashews and serve.

3 tablespoons sesame oil

1 garlic clove, crushed

2.5cm (1in) piece of fresh root ginger, finely chopped

2 Japanese aubergines, sliced

1 carrot, sliced

1 green and 1 red pepper, cut into 1cm (1/2in) dice

100g (4oz) sugarsnap peas

225g (8oz) choi sum (Chinese flowering cabbage), trimmed

12 fresh or canned water chestnuts (peeled if fresh), sliced

1 tablespoon ketjap manis *(Indonesian soy sauce)*

1 teaspoon cornflour, blended with 2 teaspoons cold water

100ml (3 1/2 fl oz) black bean sauce

75g (3oz) cashew nuts

Salt and freshly ground black pepper

Stir-fried Asian greens

In a small bowl combine the soy sauce, black vinegar, sugar, rice wine, cornflour and a pinch of salt. Set aside.

Heat a wok or large frying pan over a high heat until very hot, add the vegetable oil, then add all the greens and stir-fry for 2 minutes. Transfer to a plate and set aside.

Reheat the wok until very hot, then add the sesame oil. Add the dried chilli and peppercorns and cook for 30 seconds, until fragrant. Add the ginger and stir-fry for 10 seconds, then return the greens to the pan and toss well. Add the soy sauce mixture and cook for 1 minute, until the sauce has thickened. Serve immediately.

HOT TIP You should be able to find black vinegar in Chinese food shops. It is very dark, with a rich but mild flavour, and is used in many oriental dishes, particularly braises. If necessary, substitute white wine vinegar, or even a splash of balsamic vinegar.

1 tablespoon soy sauce

1 tablespoon Chinese black vinegar (see Hot Tip)

1/2 teaspoon sugar

1 tablespoon rice wine

1 teaspoon cornflour

1 tablespoon vegetable oil

225g (8oz) choi sum (Chinese flowering cabbage), cut into pieces

225g (8oz) pak choi, cut into pieces

225g (8oz) Chinese cabbage, shredded

1 tablespoon sesame oil

1/2 teaspoon finely chopped dried ancho chilli

6 Szechuan peppercorns, cracked (see Hot Tip on p28)

11/2 teaspoons finely grated fresh root ginger

Salt

Roasted chilli beans

Preheat the oven to 220°C/425°F/gas mark 7. Blanch the French beans in boiling salted water for 30 seconds, then drain and refresh in cold water. Drain again and dry.

Heat the oils in an ovenproof dish, add the garlic and chilli and leave over a low heat for a few

minutes to infuse. Toss the French beans in the oil, then add the soy sauce and sugar and toss again so the beans are well coated. Transfer to the oven and roast for 12–15 minutes, until the top is lightly browned. Place in a serving dish and serve immediately.

225g (8oz) French beans, trimmed

1 tablespoon vegetable oil

1/2 teaspoon sesame oil

2 garlic cloves, crushed

1 green jalapeño chilli, deseeded and finely sliced

1 tablespoon light soy sauce

1 teaspoon sugar

Horseradish and watercress mash

Cook the potatoes in boiling salted water until very tender, then drain well. Push them through a sieve to give a smooth purée, then return to a gentle heat. Add the milk and cream and beat in the butter. Mix in the horseradish and watercress, season with salt and pepper and serve.

HOT TIP This mash is also very good with 75g (3oz) mild, fresh goat's cheese beaten into it.

600g (1¼lb) floury potatoes (such as Desiree), peeled and cut into chunks

100ml (3½fl oz) full-fat milk

100ml (3½fl oz) double cream

75g (3oz) unsalted butter

1 tablespoon finely grated horse-radish root

1 bunch of watercress, stalks removed, leaves roughly chopped

Salt and freshly ground black pepper

Gratin of white roots
with horseradish

Preheat the oven to 180°C/350°F/gas mark 4. Grease a 25cm (10in) gratin dish with the butter. Cook the parsnips and turnips separately in boiling salted water for 3–4 minutes, then drain well. Season with salt, pepper and nutmeg and place in the gratin dish.

Put the double cream, milk and garlic in a pan and bring to the boil. Add the horseradish, then remove from the heat and leave to infuse for 2–3 minutes. Strain over the parsnips and turnips, ensuring that the liquid covers them. Bake for 30–40 minutes, until the vegetables are tender and the top golden.

15g (½oz) unsalted butter

400g (14oz) young parsnips, peeled and cut into large pieces

300g (10oz) young turnips, peeled but left whole

Grated nutmeg

450ml (¾ pint) double cream

150ml (¼ pint) full-fat milk

1 garlic clove, crushed

¾ teaspoon finely grated horse-radish root

Salt and freshly ground black pepper

Aztec corn

This recipe comes from central Mexico, where the Aztecs were the first people to cultivate corn, many centuries ago. there the corn is white, red or even blue in colour. Our more familiar yellow variety will do very well instead, although it is sweeter and less starchy.

When the barbecue is lit on a hot summer's day you must include this delicious and unusual dish of barbecued corn with a heady sauce of coriander, smoky chillies, lime juice, polenta and cream.

Preheat the grill. Grill the chillies about 7.5–10cm (3–4in) away from the heat, turning them regularly, until charred all over. Place them in a polythene bag and tie it up. Leave until the chillies are cool enough to handle, then peel, deseed and chop them roughly.

Melt 25g (1oz) of butter and brush onto the corn cobs. Place them under the grill – or, better still, on a barbecue – and cook, turning occasionally, for 15–20 minutes, until tender and lightly chargrilled.

Heat the remaining butter in a pan, add the spring onions and cook until softened. Stir in the coriander, chillies, lime juice, polenta and cream and simmer for 4–5 minutes or until thickened. Add the tomatoes and finally the corn. Season with salt and pepper and serve hot.

HOT TIP If you cannot find poblano chillies you could substitute green jalapeños, but remember that they are hotter.

3 green poblano chillies
50g (2oz) unsalted butter
4 corn on the cob, husks removed
4 spring onions, shredded
2 tablespoons chopped coriander
1 tablespoon lime juice
1 tablespoon polenta
150ml (1/4 pint) double cream
3 plum tomatoes, skinned, deseeded and chopped
Salt and freshly ground black pepper

Masala spinach

Heat the oil in a large pan, add the onion and fry until golden. Add the tomatoes, garlic, ground spices and chilli and fry for 5–8 minutes, until the tomatoes have reduced and the oil begins to seep out of the mixture. Add the spinach, stir, and cook over a high heat until tender. Serve immediately.

4 tablespoons vegetable oil
1 onion, finely chopped
400g (14oz) can of tomatoes, drained and chopped
1 garlic clove, crushed
1/4 teaspoon ground turmeric
1 teaspoon ground coriander
1 teaspoon ground cumin
1 green jalapeño chilli, deseeded and finely chopped
1kg (21/4lb) fresh spinach, well washed

AZTEC CORN

Barbecue french fries

These French fries have a little kick!

Cut the potatoes into chips approximately 7.5 x 1cm (3 x 1/2in). Unless you are going to cook them immediately, place in a bowl of cold water until ready to use.

Drain the potatoes in a colander and then dry in a clean cloth. Heat some vegetable oil in a deep-fat fryer or a large deep pan to 150°C/300°F and fry the chips in small batches until soft and cooked through but not coloured. Drain well.

When you are ready to serve the chips, heat the oil to 190°C/375°F and, working in batches again, fry them for about 2–3 minutes, until crisp and golden. Place in a baking tin lined with kitchen paper to absorb excess oil. Season lightly with sea salt, then add a good sprinkle of the barbecue spice mix.

900g (2lb) large potatoes (preferably Maris Piper or King Edward), peeled or well scrubbed

Vegetable oil for deep-frying

2 tablespoons Barbecue spice mix (see p157)

Sea salt

HOT TIP After the first frying, the chips can be drained and kept for several hours at room temperature before completing the cooking.

Smoky patatas bravas

For a heartier dish, I like to add sausage to this classic Spanish tapas. I prepared it this way at the hotel one day and a Spanish waiter informed me it was better than the original – a real compliment!

Boil or steam the potatoes until tender, then drain well. Heat 4 tablespoons of the oil in a large frying pan. Add the potatoes and cook over a low to moderate heat until golden all over. Remove from the pan and set aside.

Add the remaining oil to the pan with the butter, then add the onion, garlic and paprika and cook over a low heat until the onion is tender. Return the potatoes to the pan and toss with the onion mixture. Pour over the vinegar and boil until evaporated. Pour in the stock, reduce the heat and simmer until all the liquid has gone. Add the passata and chorizo and toss the whole lot together. Cover the pan and leave to cook gently for 5–8 minutes. The potatoes should be lightly sauced. Adjust the seasoning, sprinkle with the parsley and serve.

750g (1lb 10oz) waxy new potatoes, cut into large chunks

6 tablespoons virgin olive oil

25g (1oz) unsalted butter

1 onion, finely chopped

1 garlic clove, crushed

2 teaspoons Spanish smoked paprika

2 tablespoons white wine vinegar

100ml (3 1/2fl oz) chicken stock

150ml (1/4 pint) tomato passata

75g (3oz) chorizo, skinned and cut into 1cm (1/2in) dice

2 tablespoons chopped flat-leaf parsley

Salt and freshly ground black pepper

Bombay potato cake

Coarsely shred the potatoes on a mandoline, or use the coarse side of a grater. Put them in a large bowl, add the turmeric and season with salt and black pepper.

Heat a small frying pan over a high heat, add the mustard seeds and cook for about 30 seconds, until they pop. Add the oil, then stir in the curry leaves, chillies, garlic and cumin and fry for 2–3 minutes. Add to the potatoes and toss the whole lot together until well mixed. Add the coriander leaves and adjust the seasoning.

Heat the butter in a frying pan, add the potatoes and fry as one big cake. When golden underneath, invert it on to a large plate, slide it back into the pan and fry the other side until golden. Cut into wedges to serve.

450g (1lb) potatoes, peeled

1 teaspoon ground turmeric

1 teaspoon mustard seeds

2 tablespoons vegetable oil

2 curry leaves, finely chopped

2 green Thai chillies, finely chopped

1 garlic clove, crushed

1/2 teaspoon ground cumin

3 tablespoons chopped coriander

75g (3oz) unsalted butter

Salt and freshly ground black pepper

Black pepper, garlic and parsley potatoes

Preheat the oven to 190°C/375°F/gas mark 5. Peel the potatoes and slice them thinly, preferably using a mandoline. Liberally grease a large shallow baking dish with some of the butter, then arrange the potato slices, slightly overlapping, in it. Season with salt. Melt the remaining butter with the garlic and spoon some of it over the potatoes. Season all over with the cracked black pepper and then bake for about 45–50 minutes, basting from time to time with more garlic butter. When the potatoes are lightly golden and tender, remove from the oven, sprinkle over the chopped parsley and serve .

450g (1lb) medium-sized potatoes
   (preferably Desiree or King Edward)

125g (41/2oz) unsalted butter

2 garlic cloves, crushed

1–2 tablespoons finely cracked black
   pepper (see Hot Tip on 28)

2 tablespoons chopped flat-leaf parsley

Coarse salt

Chargrilled leeks
basted with mustard butter

Beat together the softened butter, mustard and lemon juice. Cook the leeks on a charcoal grill (or a ridged grill pan) until tender, basting from time to time with the mustard butter.

50g (2oz) unsalted butter, softened

1 tablespoon wholegrain mustard

1 tablespoon lemon juice

20 baby leeks, trimmed

Salt and freshly ground black pepper

Asian grilled ratatouille

I'm very fond of the original ratatouille but I love creating new versions of it, too. I find the vegetables lend themselves to piquant flavours, such as this Asian interpretation.

Mix together all the ingredients for the marinade, pour it over the vegetables and leave to marinate for at least 4 hours, preferably overnight.
Heat a barbecue or a ridged grill pan and place the vegetables on it – in batches if necessary. Cook, turning occasionally and basting with the marinade, until the vegetables are lightly charred and tender. Transfer to a large bowl, pour over the remaining marinade. Garnish with the coriander and serve.

HOT TIP Japanese aubergines are long and thin, light mauve in colour and with a sweeter flavour than the larger Mediterranean aubergines. There is no need to salt them before use. Look for them in large supermarkets, Asian shops and specialist greengrocer's.

1 Japanese aubergine, cut into slices
   1cm (1/2in) thick

2 courgettes, cut into slices 1cm
   (1/2in) thick

2 small red onions, peeled and cut into
   slices 1cm (1/2in) thick

1 red, 1 green and 1 yellow pepper,
   cut into 4cm (11/2in) dice

A handful of coriander leaves

For the marinade:

125ml (4fl oz) rice vinegar

1 tablespoon sesame oil

4 tablespoons maple syrup

Juice of 1/2 lime

2 garlic cloves, crushed

5cm (2in) piece of fresh root ginger,
   finely grated

2 jalapeño chillies, deseeded and
   finely chopped

Artichokes
with chilli aïoli

This uses baby artichokes (sometimes called *poivrade*), which are picked before the choke has formed and can be eaten whole. They are very tender, with a delicate flavour, and need hardly any preparation at all.

First prepare the aïoli: put the garlic, chillies and a little salt in a bowl. Add the egg yolks and lemon juice and beat well. Gradually add the olive oil, drop by drop at first, whisking constantly, until the mixture becomes smooth and thick. Season to taste with salt and pepper, then set aside.

For the artichokes, put the water and salt in a large pan and bring to the boil. Add the oil, then the artichokes and simmer for about 10 minutes, until the artichokes are tender (they should float to the top). Drain well, place on a serving dish and serve with the aïoli.

1 litre (1¾ pints) water

1 teaspoon salt

4 tablespoons vegetable oil

600g (1¼ lb) baby artichokes, trimmed and cut in half vertically

For the aïoli:

3 garlic cloves, crushed

2 red serrano chillies, deseeded and finely chopped

2 egg yolks

1 tablespoon lemon juice

175ml (6fl oz) olive oil

Salt and freshly ground black pepper

Chilli willies
spicy plantain chips

Plantains are a member of the banana family and are found everywhere in the Caribbean. During my time there, I saw them served in soups, vegetable dishes and salads, but my favourite way to use them is this simple, strange-sounding recipe, where they are fried and dusted with chilli powder. Served warm or cold, they make an ideal accompaniment to pre-dinner drinks.

Peel the plantains under cold running water to avoid staining your hands. Then, preferably using a mandoline, cut them lengthways into slices about 3mm (1/8in) thick. Place them in a bowl, cover with the chilli oil and leave to marinate for 1 hour.

Heat some vegetable oil in a deep-fat fryer or a large, deep saucepan to 180°C/350°F. Drop the plantain slices into the oil a few at a time and fry until golden and crisp. Drain on kitchen paper. When all the chips are done, place them in a bowl, season with salt and dust lightly with the chilli powder. Toss gently.

4 large green plantains

150ml (1/4 pint) Chilli oil (see p152)

Vegetable oil for deep-frying

1/2 teaspoon chilli powder

Salt

HOT TIP Any ground spice mix can be used as an alternative to the chilli powder – for example, Colombo, Sri Lankan or Barbecue spice mix (see pages 156–157).

ARTICHOKES WITH CHILLI AÏOLI

salads

Slow-roasted tomato salad
with Tunisian hot dressing

Preheat the oven to 110°C/225°F/gas mark 1/4. Place the tomatoes in a shallow baking tin, sprinkle over the roasted cumin and coriander seeds, sea salt, sugar and oil and roast slowly in the oven for about 25–30 minutes, until they begin to soften and dry slightly.

Meanwhile, combine all the ingredients for the dressing in a bowl and leave to stand at room temperature for the flavours to meld.

Put the warm tomatoes in a serving dish, pour over the spicy dressing and serve, either at room temperature or cold.

12 firm, small to medium plum tomatoes, halved
1/2 teaspoon each of cumin and coriander seeds, roasted in a dry frying pan
11/2 teaspoons coarse sea salt
2 teaspoons sugar
100ml (31/2fl oz) olive oil

For the dressing:
1 teaspoon Harissa (see p156)
1/2 garlic clove, crushed
1/2 red onion, finely chopped
2 tablespoons chopped coriander
Juice and zest of 1 orange
4 tablespoons groundnut oil

Roasted beetroot, feta and apricot salad

I love the combination of salty feta cheese with sweet beetroot and apricot, pepped up by a little chilli. A colourful salad with heavenly flavours.

Preheat the oven to 180°C/350°F/gas mark 4. Trim the leafy tops off the beetroot and scrub the bulbs well. Place in a baking tin, drizzle over the ground-nut oil, cover the tin with foil and bake for 1–11/2 hours, until tender. Remove from the oven and leave to cool, then peel carefully or rub off the skins. Place in a bowl.

Blanch the apricots in boiling water for 1 minute to loosen the skin, plunge into iced water, then peel them. Cut in half, remove the stone and place the apricots in a bowl.

To make the vinaigrette, mix together the vinegar, honey and chilli, whisk in both the oils and season with salt and pepper.

Dress the beetroot and the apricots with the vinaigrette (keeping them separate, otherwise the beetroot will 'bleed' into the apricots) and leave for 20 minutes to marinate. Arrange on a serving plate, sprinkle over the crumbled feta cheese and the walnuts and serve at room temperature.

900g (2lb) baby beetroot
3 tablespoons groundnut oil
450g (1lb) fresh apricots
100g (4oz) feta cheese, crumbled
2 tablespoons walnuts

For the vinaigrette:
2 teaspoons sherry vinegar
2 teaspoons honey
1 serrano chilli, thinly sliced
3 tablespoons olive oil
3 tablespoons groundnut oil
Salt and freshly ground black pepper

SLOW-ROASTED TOMATO SALAD

Roasted beetroot and basil salad
with creamed horseradish dressing

Preheat the oven to 180°C/350°F/gas mark 4. Trim the beetroot tops, leaving 2cm (3/4in) of the stalk attached. Wash them well, then wrap them in 2 foil packages, place on a baking sheet and roast for 1–11/2 hours or until tender. Unwrap the beetroot and leave until cool enough to handle.

Peel them, cut in half and place in a large bowl.

For the dressing, whisk together the soured cream or crème fraîche, horseradish, vinegar, mustard, lemon zest and some seasoning. Add the oil in a thin stream, whisking until emulsified.

Pour the dressing over the beetroot, toss well together and transfer to a salad bowl. Scatter over the basil and serve.

24 baby beetroot

6 tablespoons soured cream or crème fraîche

2 tablespoons grated horseradish root

2 tablespoons cider vinegar

2 teaspoons Dijon mustard

1/2 teaspoon grated lemon zest

6 tablespoons vegetable oil

10 basil leaves, snipped into small pieces

Salt and freshly ground black pepper

Hot and bitter salad

A simple, vibrantly coloured addition to any salad repertoire. This is great with grilled or roast chicken.

Whisk all the ingredients for the dressing together until emulsified.

Toss the salad leaves in the dressing, adjust the seasoning if necessary and serve.

A selection of hot and bitter salad leaves – choose from rocket, watercress, chicory, radicchio, dandelion, mizuna and nasturtium

For the dressing:

2 tablespoons sherry vinegar

1 teaspoon Dijon mustard

2 tablespoons walnut oil

6 tablespoons olive oil

A pinch of sugar

Salt and freshly ground black pepper

Gado gado

This is a traditional salad from Indonesia, consisting of crunchy vegetables and beansprouts with a spicy-sweet peanut dressing. Serve as a refreshing light meal or snack.

For the sauce, heat 5 tablespoons of the sesame oil in a small saucepan and fry the chilli in it until soft. In another pan, heat the peanut butter, then add the stock or water, mango chutney and coconut milk and boil for 2 minutes. Add the chilli and its oil and remove from the heat, then add the garlic, soy sauce, the remaining sesame oil and the sugar. Season to taste and add the lemon juice; the sauce may separate slightly. Keep warm.

Boil the potato until tender, drain, then peel while it is still hot. Slice and keep warm. Cook the carrots and beans separately in boiling salted water, retaining their crispness. Drain them and add to the potatoes with the cucumber and beansprouts.

To serve, season the warm vegetables. Arrange the Chinese cabbage leaves on serving plates and top with the warm vegetables and quail's eggs. Coat lightly with the sauce and serve.

HOT TIP This is also very good with the addition of some sliced tofu, fried in a little vegetable oil until golden brown.

1 waxy potato

2 carrots, cut into matchsticks

100g (4oz) French beans

75g (3oz) cucumber, cut into matchsticks

50g (2oz) beansprouts

1/2 Chinese cabbage, leaves separated

8 quail's eggs, hard-boiled, shelled and halved

Salt and freshly ground black pepper

For the peanut sauce:

6 tablespoons sesame oil

1 red Thai chilli, deseeded and finely chopped

100g (4oz) smooth peanut butter

6 tablespoons vegetable stock or water

2 tablespoons mango chutney

5 tablespoons coconut milk

1 garlic clove, crushed

1 tablespoon soy sauce

2 teaspoons brown sugar

Juice of 1 lemon

Sicilian potato and caper salad
with mustard dressing

Cook the potatoes in boiling salted water until just tender, then drain and leave until cool enough to handle. Slice them into rounds about 1cm (1/2in) thick. Then place in a bowl and add the onion, capers and oregano.

In a separate bowl, whisk together the oil, vinegar and mustard and season with salt and pepper. Pour the dressing over the potatoes and toss together. I prefer to serve this salad warm but it can also be eaten cold.

450g (1lb) waxy new potatoes, scrubbed

1 red onion, finely chopped

1 teaspoon superfine capers, rinsed and drained

1 teaspoon chopped oregano

125ml (4fl oz) extra virgin olive oil

2 tablespoons red wine vinegar

1 teaspoon Dijon mustard

Salt and freshly ground black pepper

Rujak

This refreshing hot, sweet and sour fruit salad is from Bali, where it is a popular snack. It makes a wonderful starter or an addition to any buffet. Topped with ice cream, it can also be served as an intriguing dessert.

Put the palm sugar and tamarind in a small pan with 100ml (3 1/2fl oz) of water and a pinch of salt. Boil for 2 minutes, then add the chillies and leave to infuse for a few minutes.

Place all the chopped fruit in a serving bowl and pour over the hot syrup mixture. Mix in gently and well, then leave to cool to room temperature before serving.

50g (2oz) palm sugar

2 tablespoons tamarind paste

3 red Thai chillies, deseeded and finely chopped

1 small pineapple, peeled, cored and cut into small wedges

1 green mango, peeled, stoned and sliced

1 pink grapefruit, peeled and cut into segments

1 green apple, peeled, cored and cut into 1cm (1/2in) dice

1 papaya, peeled, deseeded and cut into wedges

Salt

Spicy seafood salad

Scrub the mussels under cold running water, removing the beards and discarding any open mussels that don't close when tapped on a work surface. Place the mussels in a steamer and steam over a high heat until opened. Remove from the steamer and discard the shells.

Heat the oil in a frying pan, add the prawns and squid and fry over a high heat for 1–2 minutes only. Add the shelled mussels and place in a bowl.

Mix together all the ingredients for the dressing and pour it over the seafood. Allow to cool and serve at room temperature.

1kg (2 1/4 lb) mussels

2 tablespoons groundnut oil

450g (1lb) large raw prawns, peeled and de-veined

450g (1lb) small squid, cut into small sections

For the dressing:

2 garlic cloves, crushed

2 tablespoons finely chopped coriander

2.5cm (1in) piece of fresh root ginger, finely chopped

4 kaffir lime leaves, finely shredded

300ml (1/2 pint) unsweetened coconut cream

2 tablespoons Asian sweet chilli sauce (see p147)

Juice and zest of 1 lime

25g (1oz) coriander leaves

12 small mint leaves

Smoked eel, beetroot and apple salad
with wasabi crème fraîche

Preheat the oven to 190°C/375°F/gas mark 5. Wrap the beetroot in foil, place on a baking tray and bake for 1–1 1/2 hours, until tender. Remove from the oven and leave until cool enough to handle, then peel, slice and set aside.

Put the crème fraîche, cream, wasabi paste, lemon juice and zest, apples, onion and some salt and pepper in a bowl and mix until the cream thickens enough to coat the apple and onion. Place a 7.5cm (3in) pastry cutter on each of 4 serving plates, then arrange some beetroot slices neatly on the base. Cover with avocado slices, then some eel fillet. Top with horseradish cream, more beetroot, avocado and more horseradish cream, and finally the last of the eel fillet. Carefully remove the rings, scatter over the coriander leaves and serve.

4 medium beetroot

2 tablespoons crème fraîche

150ml (1/4 pint) double cream

1/2 teaspoon wasabi paste (Japanese horseradish)

Juice and zest of 1 lemon

2 apples, preferably Granny Smith, peeled, cored and finely diced

1 red onion, finely diced

1 avocado, peeled, stoned and cut into slices 5mm (1/4in) thick

8 large smoked eel fillets, halved

2 tablespoons coriander leaves

Salt and freshly ground black pepper

Smoked salmon and crab sushi salad
with sansho dressing

This Japanese-inspired salad uses wasabi tobiko, which is the orangey-red roe of a type of flying fish. It is available in small plastic tubs from Oriental shops, but just leave it out if you cannot find any.

Place the rice in saucepan, pour over 350ml (12fl oz) of water and quickly bring to the boil. Reduce the heat, cover and simmer until all the liquid has been absorbed. Remove from the heat and set aside for 5 minutes.

In a small pan, gently heat the vinegar and sugar. Spread the cooked rice out on a large flat tray, then sprinkle over the vinegar and sugar. Gently mix it with the rice to give a sheen to it and then leave to cool (traditionally the rice is cooled by fanning it with a cloth).

Mix the crabmeat with the salad leaves, radishes, pink ginger and hijiki, then toss with the cooled sushi rice.

Place 4 lightly oiled ring moulds or pastry cutters about 7.5cm (3in) in diameter on a tray, and line the inner edge with a band of smoked salmon. Fill the centre with the sushi salad, taking it right to the top.

Mix together all the ingredients for the dressing.

To serve, place one ring on each serving plate and then carefully remove the ring. Top each with a little wasabi tobiko, if using and pour a little of the dressing around.

HOT TIP For me, hijiki is the tastiest of all seaweeds. It is full of iodine and essential minerals and has a pleasant, chewy texture. There is no need to soak it before using. You should be able to find it in Japanese food shops or health food shops.

150g (5oz) short grain rice, rinsed

1 tablespoon rice vinegar

2 teaspoons sugar

125g (4½oz) fresh white crabmeat

100g (4oz) mixed bitter salad leaves, such as peashoots, dandelion, mizuna and frisée, torn into small pieces

4 red radishes, thinly sliced

1 tablespoon pickled pink ginger, shredded

15g (½oz) hijiki seaweed

225g (8oz) thinly sliced smoked salmon

1 tablespoon wasabi tobiko (optional)

For the dressing:

½ teaspoon sansho (Japanese pepper)

2 tablespoons red wine vinegar

2 tablespoons light soy sauce

4 tablespoons sesame oil

4 tablespoons vegetable oil

Juice of ½ lemon

2 teaspoons Asian sweet chilli sauce (see p147)

Seared tuna tartare
and noodle salad

This simple and impressive salad is ideal for summer. Light in flavour and texture, it can be prepared well in advance and put together when needed. Be sure to use very, very fresh tuna, as it is barely cooked.

Cut the tuna fillet into neat 2cm (3/4in) dice and place in a bowl. Add the sweet chilli sauce, half the sesame oil, plus the garlic and ginger, then cover and chill for 2 hours.

Mix together all the ingredients for the dressing and set aside.

Place the noodles in a large bowl and pour over enough boiling water to cover them. Leave for 1 minute and then drain in a colander.

Heat the remaining sesame oil in a wok or a large frying pan over a high heat. Add the tuna and its marinating juices and toss for about 30 seconds to seal. Remove from the pan and set aside. Add all the vegetables to the pan and stir-fry for 1 minute or until just cooked and still crunchy. Return the tuna to the pan with the vegetables, add the noodles and toss well. Pour over the dressing and pile on to serving plates. Sprinkle over some black sesame seeds and coriander leaves and serve immediately.

450g (1lb) sushi-quality fresh tuna fillet

3 tablespoons Asian sweet chilli sauce (see p147)

4 tablespoons sesame oil

1 garlic clove, crushed

2.5cm (1in) piece of fresh root ginger, cut into fine strips

300g (11oz) egg thread noodles

75g (3oz) beansprouts

1 red pepper, cut into fine strips

1/4 cucumber, deseeded and cut into fine strips

1 bunch of choi sum (Chinese flowering cabbage), trimmed

50g (2oz) mizuna (oriental mustard leaf)

Black sesame seeds and coriander leaves, to garnish

For the dressing:

1 teaspoon caster sugar

2 teaspoons rice vinegar

2 tablespoons nam pla (Thai fish sauce)

2 tablespoons dark soy sauce

Juice of 1 lime

Grilled squid and melon salad
with hot and sour kaffir dressing

What I like about this salad is the combination of chewy fish and tangy, lightly chargrilled fruit. It makes a wonderful starter for a summer dinner.

Slit the squid bodies open, cut them into large rectangles and then score in a diamond pattern on the inner side with a sharp knife (this makes them curl up attractively when cooked). Leave the tentacles in large pieces. Mix all the marinade ingredients together in a large bowl, add the squid and melon and leave to marinate at room temperature for 2–3 hours.

Heat the grill to its highest setting. Remove the squid and melon from the marinade, place on the grill pan and grill for 4–5 minutes. Transfer to a bowl and sprinkle over the herbs.

Put all the ingredients for the dressing into a pan and heat gently. Pour the dressing over the squid and melon. Leave to cool to room temperature before serving.

225g (8oz) cleaned squid

1/4 honeydew melon, peeled and cut into thin wedges

A slice of watermelon, peeled and cut into thin wedges

1 tablespoon roughly chopped mint leaves

1 tablespoon roughly chopped coriander leaves

For the marinade:

100ml (31/2fl oz) olive oil

1/4 teaspoon chilli powder

1 garlic clove

Juice of 1 lime

2 tablespoons sugar

For the dressing:

3 tablespoons nam pla (Thai fish sauce)

2 tablespoons lime juice

1 garlic clove, crushed

1 red and 1 green chilli, deseeded and finely chopped

1 teaspoon brown sugar

4 kaffir lime leaves, finely shredded

Peppered chicken liver salad
with gorgonzola dressing

This salad crosses several different flavour spectrums – tangy, sweet and slightly hot. The creamy bite of the gorgonzola makes a perfect foil for the chicken livers.

For the dressing, put the cheese and hot water in a bowl and crush it to a smooth purée with a fork. Stir in the vinegar, then add the crème fraîche and lemon juice and season to taste. Add the chives.

Cook the sugarsnaps and French beans separately in boiling salted water. Drain, refresh under cold running water and drain again.

Wrap the peppercorns in a tea towel and place on a work surface. Using a hammer or rolling pin, crack the peppercorns. Place on a plate, add the cleaned chicken livers and roll them in the pepper.

Season with a little salt.

Heat the oil in a frying pan until nearly smoking. Add half the chicken livers in a single layer and cook for 1 minute on each side, until coloured. Transfer to a plate and keep warm while you cook the remaining livers. Place the leaves in a large bowl, add all the vegetables except the cherry tomatoes and toss with the gorgonzola dressing. Pile the salad up on 4 serving plates. Top with the peppered chicken livers and garnish with the cherry tomato halves.

75g (3oz) sugarsnap peas

75g (3oz) fine French beans

1 teaspoon black peppercorns

350g (12oz) fresh chicken livers, cleaned

4 tablespoons vegetable oil

100g (4oz) mixed green salad leaves

2 medium carrots, cut into fine strips

6 cherry tomatoes, halved

Salt and freshly ground black pepper

For the gorgonzola dressing:

50g (2oz) gorgonzola cheese

4 tablespoons hot water

1 tablespoon champagne vinegar

125ml (4fl oz) crème fraîche

Juice of 1/2 lemon

2 tablespoons chopped chives

Creole chicken salad
with blackbeans, corn and oregano–hot pepper vinaigrette

Season the chicken breasts with salt and a little pepper and then dust with the spice mix. Fry them in a little hot oil – or chargrill them, which I think is better!

While the chicken is cooking, make the vinaigrette: place the wine vinegar, mustard and garlic in a bowl, then whisk in the oil a little at a time.

Add the Tabasco, lemon juice and oregano.

Place the salad leaves, cooked beans, sweetcorn and tomatoes in a large bowl, pour over the vinaigrette and toss well together. Season to taste. Cut the hot chicken into 2cm (3/4in) dice and scatter on top of the salad, then serve immediately – a wonderful blend of hot and cold.

4 x 200g (7oz) chicken breasts, boned and skinned

2 tablespoons Blackened Cajun spice mix (see p157)

Oil for frying (optional)

1 head of chicory, leaves separated

2 romaine (Cos) or Little Gem lettuces, leaves separated

1 bunch of watercress

75g (3oz) black beans, cooked

4 tablespoons sweetcorn

12 cherry tomatoes, halved

Salt and freshly ground black pepper

For the vinaigrette:

2 tablespoons white wine vinegar

2 teaspoons Dijon mustard

1 garlic clove, crushed

125ml (4fl oz) olive oil

4 drops of Tabasco sauce

1 teaspoon lemon juice

1 teaspoon chopped oregano

Warm steak salad
with horseradish, mustard and balsamic juices

For the dressing, place the mustard, horseradish and garlic in a bowl, add the vinegar and leave for 10–15 minutes to infuse. Whisk in the oil to form a dressing. Season with salt and pepper and then add the coriander.

Heat the vegetable oil in a small frying pan until almost smoking. Season the beef fillet with salt and pepper, add to the pan and fry over a moderate heat for 8–10 minutes, turning once (alternatively cook in a hot oven for 5–8 minutes); this should give medium-rare to medium meat.

Remove from the pan and keep warm.

Return the pan in which the meat was cooked to the heat and add the meat stock. Bring to the boil and boil for 1 minute, stirring and scraping the bottom of the pan to deglaze, then add to the dressing and mix thoroughly.

Place the salad leaves and vegetable strips in a bowl and toss with half the dressing. Put the salad in a serving dish. Slice the beef fillet thinly and arrange on top of the salad. Pour on the remaining dressing and serve.

2 tablespoons vegetable oil

450g (1lb) best-quality beef fillet

150g (5oz) bag of mixed salad leaves

1 large carrot, cut into strips 3mm
  (1/8in) thick

1/2 celeriac, cut into strips 3mm
  (1/8in) thick

1 large beetroot, cut into strips 3mm
  (1/8in) thick

1 red onion, thinly sliced

Salt and freshly ground black pepper

For the dressing:

1 teaspoon Dijon mustard

1 teaspoon grated horseradish root

1 garlic clove, crushed

4 tablespoons balsamic vinegar

125ml (4fl oz) vegetable oil

1 tablespoon chopped coriander

100ml (3 1/2fl oz) meat stock

pasta, rice and bread

BUCATINI WITH CLAMS, GARLIC AND CHORIZO

Bucatini
with clams, garlic and chorizo

Scrub the clams under cold running water, discarding any open ones that don't close when tapped on a work surface. Set aside.

Cook the pasta in a large pan of boiling salted water until *al dente*.

Meanwhile, heat half the oil in a large pan over a medium heat, add the garlic and cook for 1 minute without letting it colour. Stir in the parsley, then add the clams and pour over the white wine. Cover with a lid and leave to steam for 2 minutes. Add the tomatoes, chilli and chorizo and pour over the remaining olive oil. Cover again and leave to cook for a further 2 minutes, until the clams open.

Drain the pasta. Stir the clam and chorizo sauce, then toss with the pasta and serve immediately into individual bowls.

HOT TIP The bucatini could be replaced by another long pasta, such as spaghetti or fettuccine. For a real treat, you could also add some more shellfish to the sauce – mussels and cockles would be good.

48 baby venus clams

450g (1lb) bucatini pasta

6 tablespoons olive oil

2 garlic cloves, crushed

1 tablespoon finely chopped flat-leaf parsley

5 tablespoons dry white wine

400g (14oz) can of tomatoes, chopped

1/2 teaspoon finely chopped dried peperoncino chilli

75g (3oz) chorizo, outer casing removed, cut into 5mm (1/4in) dice

Fried ginger noodles
with pak choi and spring onions

Place the noodles in a large bowl and pour over enough boiling water to cover. Leave for 30 seconds, then drain in a colander.

Heat the vegetable oil in a wok or a large frying pan, add the ginger and garlic, then add the pak choi leaves and stir-fry for 1 minute. Add the drained noodles, oyster sauce, soy and fish sauce and mix well together.

Serve immediately, sprinkled with the shredded spring onions.

450g (1lb) egg thread noodles

2 tablespoons vegetable oil

2.5cm (1in) piece of fresh root ginger, finely chopped

1 garlic clove, crushed

4 pak choi, separated into leaves

2 tablespoons oyster sauce

1 tablespoon dark soy sauce

1 teaspoon nam pla (Thai fish sauce)

4 spring onions, finely shredded

Wok-fried noodles
with dry-spiced beef

Bring 2 litres (3½ pints) of water to the boil, add the beef and poach for 1 hour or until it is so tender that the meat fibres separate easily. Leave to cool a little and then shred it finely with a fork.

Put the garlic, palm sugar, chillies, galangal, shrimp paste and ground cloves in a blender or food processor and blitz to a coarse paste. Heat the oil in a frying pan and cook the paste over a moderate heat for 2–3 minutes, until fragrant. Add the finely shredded beef, mix well and sauté until the moisture from the spice paste has evaporated and the meat is tacky. Season to taste.

Place the noodles in a bowl, pour over plenty of boiling salted water and leave for 30 seconds to swell. Drain them well, toss with the spiced beef and serve immediately.

350g (12oz) beef skirt

1 tablespoon crushed garlic

1 tablespoon palm sugar

2 red Thai chillies, deseeded and finely chopped

2.5cm (1in) piece of fresh galangal (or root ginger), peeled and finely sliced

2 teaspoons blachan (dried shrimp paste)

½ teaspoon ground cloves

2 tablespoons vegetable oil

450g (1lb) egg thread noodles

Salt and freshly ground black pepper

Steamed Chinese cabbage wraps

A type of Asian dolmades, this makes a wonderful side dish or starter. Vegetarians could replace the fish sauce with light soy sauce.

Heat the oil in a pan, add the diced aubergine and fry over a moderate heat until golden and tender. Lower the heat, add the onion, garlic and lemongrass and cook for 3–4 minutes, until the onion is softened. Transfer to a bowl, add the cooked rice, tomatoes and herbs, then season with the fish sauce and sweet chilli sauce. Leave to marinate for at least 4 hours, preferably overnight.

Using a sharp knife, carefully remove at least a third of the stem from each Chinese cabbage leaf.

Blanch the leaves in boiling salted water for 30 seconds, then transfer to a bowl of iced water using a slotted spoon. Put the leaves on a cloth to drain and then lay them out on a board.

Place 2 good heaped tablespoons of the filling at the base of each leaf and roll up, folding in the sides. To serve, reheat in a steamer or place in an ovenproof dish with about 100ml (3½fl oz) water, cover with foil and warm through in the oven. Serve with a little warm sweet chilli sauce.

HOT TIP Add some cooked prawns or lobster to the filling.

100ml (3½fl oz) vegetable oil

1 aubergine, finely diced

1 onion, finely chopped

1 garlic clove, crushed

1 tablespoon finely chopped lemongrass

150g (5oz) cooked sushi or basmati rice

6 medium tomatoes, skinned, deseeded and diced

½ tablespoon roughly chopped mint

1 tablespoon roughly chopped coriander

1 tablespoon roughly chopped basil

3 tablespoons nam pla (Thai fish sauce)

6 tablespoons Asian sweet chilli sauce (see p147), plus extra to serve

8 large outer leaves of Chinese cabbage

Bigoli
with spicy meat sauce

Bigoli is a thick wholewheat spaghetti from Venice, usually served with robust sauces such as anchovy and onion, or this spicy mixture of minced pork and chicken livers. If you can't find bigoli, bucatini makes a good substitute.

Season the pork with salt and pepper. Heat 4 tablespoons of the oil in a heavy-based frying pan, then add the pork and cook over a high heat until sealed all over. Stir in the vegetables, garlic and chilli flakes and cook for 2–3 minutes. Add the diced chicken livers, cover the pan and cook for 5 minutes, then pour in the red wine, cover again and cook for 2 minutes longer. Stir in the tomato purée, passata, sugar and a little salt, then reduce the heat, cover and cook for about 20–30 minutes, stirring occasionally.

Cook the pasta in plenty of boiling salted water until al dente, then drain well. Toss the pasta with the remaining oil and some nutmeg, salt and pepper. Add the meat sauce and chopped sage, toss together, then serve.

HOT TIP It's a myth that you need to add oil to the cooking water to prevent pasta sticking. Just cook the pasta in plenty of boiling water until *al dente* and it will be fine. Once it has been drained, toss it in a little oil to help keep the strands separate.

350g (12oz) minced pork

6 tablespoons olive oil

1 onion, finely chopped

1 carrot, finely chopped

1 celery stick, finely chopped

1 garlic clove, finely chopped

1 teaspoon dried red chilli flakes

100g (4oz) chicken livers, cleaned and
  finely diced

150ml (1/4 pint) red wine

2 tablespoons tomato purée

150ml (1/4 pint) tomato passata

A pinch of sugar

450g (1lb) bigoli pasta

Grated nutmeg

1 tablespoon chopped sage

Salt and freshly ground black pepper

Mushroom pad thai

Pad Thai is one of many noodle stir-fries prepared throughout the Far East. I first experienced it during a trip to Thailand, where it is practically a national dish. It is usually made with dried rice vermicelli but any oriental noodle is fine – even an Italian pasta such as linguine would do at a pinch.

Soak the noodles in plenty of cold water for 10 minutes, then drain. Cook in a large pan of boiling salted water for 5 minutes, then drain, refresh under cold running water and drain again thoroughly.

Heat half the oil in a wok or a large frying pan, add the garlic, chillies and shiitake mushrooms and fry for 2–3 minutes, until the mushrooms are browned all over. Add the noodles and toss with the mush-rooms, then add the fish sauce and soy sauce and mix well. Remove the mixture from the wok and keep warm.

Wipe out the wok and heat the remaining oil in it. Add the beaten eggs and cook until lightly scram-bled. Return the noodles to the pan, mix well and season with salt and pepper to taste. Turn out on to a serving dish and sprinkle with the spring onions, coriander leaves and peanuts.

450g (1lb) rice noodles

2 tablespoons vegetable or groundnut oil

3 garlic cloves, crushed

2 serrano chillies, thinly sliced

300g (10oz) shiitake mushrooms, thickly
  sliced

1 tablespoon nam pla (Thai fish sauce)

2 tablespoons ketjap manis (Indonesian
  soy sauce)

2 eggs, beaten

4 spring onions, thinly shredded

2 tablespoons coriander leaves

4 tablespoons roasted peanuts, chopped

Salt and freshly ground black pepper

Shiitake and butternut squash orzotto
with chilli pecorino

Orzo is a rice-shaped pasta, which I have used here instead of rice to make a sort of risotto – or orzotto. Coincidentally, after devising this recipe I discovered that you could buy pecorino cheese with chilli in it. If you manage to find some, cut it into fine shavings and substitute it for the grated pecorino. Either cut down the amount of jalapeño or leave it out entirely, depending on your chilli tolerance – the chilli pecorino is surprisingly strong.

Heat the olive oil in a heavy-based pan, add the garlic and spring onions and cook for 1 minute. Add the orzo and cook for a further minute, stirring to coat the pasta with the oil and garlic. Stir in the squash and cook for 5 minutes. Meanwhile, bring the stock to the boil in a separate pan and keep at simmering point.

Add the stock to the orzo a little at a time, stirring occasionally and making sure the pasta is always just covered by the liquid. After 10 minutes, add the shiitake, then continue adding the stock until the orzo is *al dente*. Remove the pan from the heat, stir in the butter and season with salt and black pepper to taste.

Mix together the cheese, chilli and mint, scatter on top of the pasta and serve immediately.

2 tablespoons virgin olive oil

1 garlic clove, crushed

4 spring onions, shredded on the diagonal

450g (1lb) orzo pasta

1 small butternut squash, peeled, deseeded and cut into 1cm (1/2in) cubes

1 litre (13/4 pints) well-flavoured chicken or vegetable stock

12 shiitake mushrooms, thickly sliced

15g (1/2oz) unsalted butter

2 tablespoons grated pecorino cheese

1 jalapeño chilli, deseeded and finely chopped

1 tablespoon chopped mint

Salt and freshly ground black pepper

Paprika pasta paella

This is based on *fideua*, a classic paella from Valencia made with noodles instead of rice. Here I've used lumachine ('little snails') pasta.

Put the stock and saffron in a pan and bring to the boil, then remove from the heat and set aside.

Heat the oil in a separate pan, add the onion, chilli flakes and garlic and fry over a moderate heat for 5 minutes, until golden. Stir in the paprika. Add the aubergine, red pepper and artichokes and stir to coat with the paprika, then add the tomatoes.

Lower the heat and cook for 5–8 minutes. Add the hot stock and bring to the boil, then add the pasta and spread it out evenly. Season with salt and pepper, reduce the heat and cook for 12–15 minutes. Taste the noodles to check they are cooked, then remove from the heat and allow to rest for a few minutes before serving.

900ml (1½ pints) vegetable or chicken stock
½ teaspoon saffron strands
4 tablespoons olive oil
1 onion, finely chopped
1 teaspoon dried red chilli flakes
1 garlic clove, crushed
1 tablespoon hot Hungarian paprika
1 aubergine, cut into 1cm (½in) dice
1 red pepper, cut into 1cm (½in) dice
2 prepared artichoke hearts
400g (14oz) can of chopped tomatoes
450g (1lb) lumachine pasta
50g (2oz) French beans, cooked
Salt and freshly ground black pepper

Hot pepper peanut rice

I love the warm, ochre colour of this spicy rice, which makes a good accompaniment to just about any grilled meat or fish.

Heat the chilli oil and butter in a pan, add the garlic, onion, carrot, celery and red pepper and cook over a moderate heat for 2 minutes. Add the dried chilli flakes and rice and cook for 2–3 minutes, until the rice takes on a red, shiny glaze. Add the

chicken stock or water and bring to the boil, stirring occasionally, then add the bay leaf. Reduce the heat, cover the pan and cook for 12–15 minutes or until the rice is tender and has absorbed the liquid. Stir in the peanuts, adjust the seasoning and serve.

2 tablespoons Chilli oil (see p152)
25g (1oz) unsalted butter
2 garlic cloves, crushed
½ onion, finely diced
1 carrot, finely diced
1 celery stick, finely diced
1 red pepper, finely diced
1 teaspoon dried red chilli flakes
225g (8oz) long grain rice
450ml (¾ pint) chicken stock or water
1 bay leaf
75g (3oz) unsalted peanuts
Salt and freshly ground black pepper

* Penne arrabbiatta

'Angry pasta' is a classic Italian dish that uses a little dried chilli to spice up a simple tomato sauce. Parmesan lovers may wish to top it with a little Parmesan, although this is not traditional. I find it robs the dish of its heady power.

To make the sauce, heat the oil in a pan, add the chilli flakes and garlic and cook over a low heat for 1 minute. Add the passata and bring to the boil, then reduce the heat and simmer until reduced by half.

Cook the pasta in plenty of boiling salted water until *al dente*. Drain well and toss with the butter, then season with salt and pepper. Toss the sauce with the pasta and serve straight away.

2 tablespoons olive oil

*1 teaspoon dried red chilli flakes
(or hot chilli paste)*

4 garlic cloves, crushed

200ml (7fl oz) tomato passata

450g (1lb) penne

25g (1oz) unsalted butter

Salt and freshly ground black pepper

Trenette frittata
with peperone and venus clams

Scrub the clams under cold running water, discarding any open ones that don't close when tapped on a work surface. Put them in a large pan, pour over the white wine, then cover and place on a high heat for 1–2 minutes, until the clams open. Drain in a colander, then strain the juices through a fine sieve and reserve. Shell the clams and set aside.

Heat 3 tablespoons of the olive oil in a small frying pan, add the garlic and cook over a low heat until softened. Add the red pepper, dried chilli flakes and peperone slices and cook until the pepper is softened. Then add the clams and their juice and cook for 1 minute. Remove the pan from the heat and set aside.

Cook the pasta in plenty of boiling salted water until *al dente*, then drain well. In a bowl, toss the pasta with the clam and pepper mixture and leave to cool.

Add the beaten eggs and the parsley to the cooled pasta mixture and season with salt and pepper. In a small frying pan or omelette pan (preferably non-stick), heat the remaining oil. Add the pasta mixture and spread it out with a fork. Reduce the heat and, stirring carefully from time to time, cook until browned underneath and just set. Place a large plate over the pan and invert the frittata on to it. Slide the frittata, browned-side up, back into the pan and cook on the other side for 2 minutes. Turn out on to a serving plate and leave to cool slightly before cutting into wedges to serve.

30 small venus clams

125ml (4fl oz) dry white wine

6 tablespoons olive oil

3 garlic cloves, crushed

1 red pepper, cut into 5mm (1/4in) dice

1/2 teaspoon dried red chilli flakes

*75g (3oz) peperone, cut into slices
2.5cm (1in) thick*

250g (9oz) trenette (linguine)

5 large eggs, lightly beaten

1 tablespoon chopped flat-leaf parsley

Salt and freshly ground black pepper

HOT TIP If you are not feeling brave enough to turn the frittata over to cook the other side, simply put the pan under a hot grill until the mixture is just set and lightly coloured.

SAFFRON AND MUSTARD SEED RICE

Saffron and mustard seed rice

Put the water, salt, lemon juice and zest and saffron in a pan and bring to the boil, then leave to infuse for 5 minutes over a very low heat.

Heat the ghee or vegetable oil in another pan, large enough to take the rice, add the mustard seeds and sauté until they pop and become aromatic. Add the rice and stir to mix with the seeds.

Cook for 1 minute, then add the saffron-infused water. Bring to the boil, reduce the heat and cover with a tight-fitting lid. Cook gently for about 15 minutes, until the rice is tender and fluffy.

Remove from the heat and leave, covered, for 5 minutes to allow the rice to steam. Transfer to a serving dish and drizzle over the Indian chilli oil.

600ml (1 pint) water

1/2 teaspoon salt

Juice and zest of 1/2 lemon

1 teaspoon saffron strands

2 tablespoons ghee or vegetable oil

2 teaspoons black mustard seeds

250g (9oz) basmati rice, well washed and drained

2 tablespoons Indian chilli oil (see p152)

Hoppin' John

In America's Deep South, this dish of rice and black-eyed peas is eaten at the New Year to bring good luck. If you cannot find black-eyed peas, substitute another type of bean such as kidney or cannellini, but don't expect such good luck if you do!

   Although it's not traditional, I find cooking the rice separately from the peas keeps the dish better defined. When they are cooked together, the rice loses its texture.

Heat the oil in a pan, add the bacon and fry for 5 minutes, until lightly coloured. Add the onion, garlic, celery, red pepper and paprika and cook for 2 minutes. Add the soaked black-eyed peas and cover with the stock. Bring to the boil, then reduce the heat and cook for about 30 minutes or until the

peas are tender.

Meanwhile, cook the rice in plenty of boiling salted water, then drain well. Stir the black-eyed pea mixture into the rice, add the spring onions and hot pepper sauce and season to taste. Sprinkle over the cheese, if using, and serve straight away.

2 tablespoons vegetable oil

250g (9oz) piece of smoked bacon, cut into small pieces

1 onion, chopped

2 garlic cloves, crushed

1 celery stick, chopped

1 red pepper, finely chopped

1 teaspoon smoked paprika

300g (10oz) black-eyed peas, soaked overnight and then drained

1 litre (13/4 pints) chicken stock

125g (41/2oz) long grain rice

4 spring onions, finely shredded

1 teaspoon West Indian hot pepper sauce

75g (3oz) sharp Cheddar cheese, grated (optional)

Salt and freshly ground black pepper

Smoked fish kedgeree
with scrambled eggs

Heat half the butter in a heavy-based saucepan, add the onion and mushrooms and cook over a low heat for 5–6 minutes, until softened. Stir in the curry paste and cook for 1 minute. Add the cooked rice and stir until well coated in the butter. Add the smoked salmon, cooked smoked haddock and peas and season lightly. Keep warm.

In a separate pan, heat the remaining butter and the cream, season with salt and pepper and then pour in the beaten eggs. Scramble them over a very low heat, keeping them soft and light in texture. Fold the eggs carefully into the rice and transfer to a serving plate. Sprinkle over the chopped parsley and serve.

50g (2oz) unsalted butter
1 small onion, finely chopped
75g (3oz) button mushrooms, sliced
1½ teaspoons My curry paste (see p154)
225g (8oz) basmati rice, cooked
100g (4oz) smoked salmon, cut into slivers
350g (12oz) smoked haddock, cooked and flaked
50g (2oz) peas, cooked
6 tablespoons double cream
4 eggs, beaten
1 tablespoon chopped parsley
Salt and freshly ground black pepper

Hot and sour yoghurt rice

Wash the rice well, cover with cold water and leave to soak for 1 hour. Drain well, then place in a heavy-based saucepan, add a little salt and level off the rice. Pour in enough water to cover the rice by 2.5–5cm (1–2in). Bring to the boil, cover with a tight-fitting lid and reduce the heat to low. Leave undisturbed for about 20 minutes, until all the liquid has been absorbed and the rice is tender.

Meanwhile, heat the oil in a frying pan, add the vegetables, garlic, chillies, cumin and dried herbs and cook for 4–5 minutes, until soft. Place in a blender, add the coriander leaves, lime juice, yoghurt and 150ml (1/4 pint) of water and blitz to a coarse purée. Return to the pan to reheat, then season with salt and pepper.

Fluff up the rice with a fork to separate the grains and release trapped steam. Add the yoghurt spice mix, folding in carefully. Serve hot or cold.

450g (1lb) basmati rice
2 tablespoons groundnut oil
1 celery stick, chopped
1 onion, chopped
2 green peppers, chopped
4 garlic cloves, crushed
3 jalapeño chillies, deseeded and chopped
1 teaspoon ground cumin
1 teaspoon dried thyme
1 teaspoon dried oregano
A good handful of coriander leaves
Juice of 2 limes
150ml (1/4 pint) yoghurt
Salt and freshly ground black pepper

SMOKED FISH KEDGEREE

Jalapeño cornbread

Preheat the oven to 190°C/375°F/gas mark 5. Combine the flour, polenta, salt, baking powder and sugar in a mixing bowl and make a well in the centre. Add the beaten eggs, melted butter and milk and mix well to form a smooth batter. Stir in the chilli, sweetcorn and grated cheese. Pour the mixture into a lightly greased 20cm (8in) cake tin or cast-iron frying pan and smooth the surface. Bake for 25 minutes, until golden and firm to the touch. Allow to cool in the tin a little, then turn out and serve warm, cut into small squares or wedges, with butter.

150g (5oz) plain flour

150g (5oz) fine polenta

A pinch of salt

4 teaspoons baking powder

50g (2oz) caster sugar

2 eggs, beaten

1 tablespoon melted unsalted butter

250ml (8fl oz) full-fat milk

1 green jalapeño chilli, deseeded and finely chopped

200g (7oz) can of sweetcorn kernels, drained

225g (8oz) Cheddar cheese, grated

Asian-style focaccia

We always serve a variety of breads at the Lanesborough and I invented this one as a means of using my favourite flavourings – coriander, pickled ginger and sweet chilli. It's been very popular and is surprisingly easy to make.

Sift the flour and salt into a large mixing bowl and stir in the yeast. Mix together 4 tablespoons of oil, the water, garlic, ginger and coriander and stir into the flour to form a rough dough. Turn the dough out on to a floured surface and knead until smooth and elastic. Place in a lightly oiled bowl, cover with clingfilm and leave to rise at room temperature for 1–1 1/2 hours, until almost double in size.
Preheat the oven to 200°C/400°F/gas mark 6. Turn out the dough and knead lightly to knock out the air, then roll out to a square, about 2cm (3/4in) thick. Place in a well-greased 25–30cm (10–12in) cake tin or on a baking sheet. Using floured fingers, make indentations at 2.5cm (1in) intervals all over the dough. Drizzle over the remaining olive oil, then bake for about 25–30 minutes, until golden in colour and spongy in texture.
Blend the chilli sauce and vegetable oil together and brush it over the surface of the bread two or three times. Serve warm or cold.

675g (1 1/2 lb) strong white flour
1 tablespoon salt
1 sachet of fast-action easy-blend dried yeast
450ml (3/4 pint) lukewarm water
6 tablespoons olive oil
1 garlic clove, crushed
3 tablespoons pickled pink ginger, dried in a cloth, roughly chopped
4 tablespoons roughly chopped coriander
6 tablespoons Asian sweet chilli sauce (see p147)
3 tablespoons vegetable oil

HOT TIP The dough can be used as a pizza base and baked with your favourite toppings.

Mediterranean chilli, olive and cumin fougasse

Sift the flour and salt into a large mixing bowl and stir in the yeast. Mix together the water, 4 tablespoons of the olive oil, the garlic, chillies, olives and cumin seeds and stir into the flour to form a rough dough. Turn the dough out on to a floured surface and knead until smooth and elastic. Place in a lightly oiled bowl, cover with clingfilm and leave to rise at room temperature for 1–11/2 hours, until almost doubled in size.

Turn out the dough and knead lightly to knock out the air, then roll out to a rectangle about 1cm (1/2in) thick. Cut the rectangle in half diagonally to form 2 triangles. Cover loosely with clingfilm to prevent a skin forming and leave to rest for 20 minutes.

Preheat the oven to 200°C/400°F/gas mark 6. Now lightly stretch the triangles a little by hand or with a rolling pin, maintaining the triangle shape. Dust lightly with flour and then, with a sharp knife, cut 3 or 4 slashes in each triangle, ensuring you cut right through the dough.

Line a large baking sheet with baking parchment and carefully transfer the triangles to it, stretching them to open out the slashes. Bake for 20 minutes, until golden brown and spongy. Restrain yourself until the fougasse has cooled a little before devouring it!

675g (11/2lb) strong white flour

15g (1/2oz) salt

1 sachet of fast-action easy-blend dried yeast

450ml (3/4 pint) lukewarm water

6 tablespoons olive oil

1 garlic clove, crushed

2 serrano chillies, deseeded and chopped

150g (5oz) black olives, stoned and roughly chopped

2 teaspoons cumin seeds, toasted in a dry frying pan

HOT TIP Make the fougasse using spicy olives from a deli and omit the chillies and cumin.

Grilled black pepper naans

Naan is a Punjabi bread, usually baked in tandoor clay ovens to give a wonderful charred flavour. Unfortunately most of us do not have tandoor ovens but the baking can be done in the oven or, as here, under a hot grill. This recipe is adapted from Linda Collister's wonderful *Bread Book*.

Heat a small frying pan over a moderate heat, add the black pepper and keep it moving for 20 seconds, until it gives off its peppery fragrance. Remove from the pan and set aside.

Put the flour, yoghurt and salt in a bowl and add 125ml (4fl oz) warm water a little at a time, working it into the flour with your fingers until it forms a slightly sticky dough. Lightly mix in the ground coriander and black pepper. Knead for a few seconds, then cover with a damp cloth and leave at room temperature for 1-11/4 hours.

To cook, preheat the grill to its highest setting. Flour your hands, pull off small pieces of the dough and shape each one into a ball. Roll out on a floured surface into an oval shape about 15–20cm (6–8in) long. Place the naans under the hot grill until they puff up and char-blister; this shouldn't take more than 40 seconds. Turn them over and cook on the second side, keep warm while the others cook. Serve warm.

HOT TIP It's worth experimenting with all manner of spices for these naans – cumin, fenugreek, turmeric and nigella, for example.

Makes 8

1 teaspoon cracked black peppercorns
(see Hot Tip on p28)
250g (9oz) self-raising flour
2 tablespoons Greek yoghurt
1 teaspoon salt
1 teaspoon ground coriander

Quick garlic chilli bread

Preheat the grill to its highest setting. In a blender, blitz together the garlic, harissa, oil and basil until smooth. Brush a generous amount of this paste over each slice of baguette. Place on a baking tray, sprinkle with the cheese and place under the grill until golden and bubbling. Serve hot.

3 garlic cloves, crushed
2 tablespoons Harissa (see p156)
100ml (3 1/2 fl oz) olive oil
A good handful of basil leaves
1 baguette, cut into slices 2.5cm
(1in) thick
1 tablespoon grated Cheddar cheese

Minced lamb and feta pide

Pide is a sort of Turkish pizza, with a spicy lamb topping rather like a kofta mix. I like to drizzle some yoghurt mixed with grated onion and chopped mint over it just before serving, to temper the heat of the spicy lamb.

Sift the flour and salt into a mixing bowl, make a well in the centre and put the potato in it. Put the yeast and sugar in a small bowl, pour on the tepid water and mix thoroughly until dissolved. Mix the yeast mixture slowly into the potato and flour and then turn out and knead to a soft and pliable dough, adding a little more water if necessary. Place in a lightly oiled bowl, cover with a damp cloth and leave to rise at room temperature for 1–11/2 hours.

For the filling, heat the oil in a heavy-based saucepan, add the minced lamb and fry until browned all over. Add the onion, chilli and garlic and cook for 1 minute. Add the tomato purée and spices and cook for 2 minutes, then stir in 150ml (1/4 pint) of water. Bring to the boil, then lower the heat and cook for 10-12 minutes, until reduced and thick. Leave to cool.

Preheat oven to 190°C/375°F/gas mark 5 and place a large baking sheet in it to heat up. Knock back the dough, divide in half and roll out each piece into a round about 23cm (9in) in diameter. Brush with the olive oil. Spread the cooled lamb mixture on top, scatter over the feta cheese and bake in the oven on the hot baking tray for about 10–12 minutes, until the base is crisp. Serve warm.

225g (8oz) strong white flour, sifted

1 teaspoon salt

75g (3oz) mashed potato (unseasoned)

15g (1/2oz) fresh yeast

1 teaspoon sugar

125ml (4fl oz) lukewarm water

2 tablespoons olive oil

For the filling:

3 tablespoons olive oil

350g (12oz) lean minced lamb

1 onion, finely chopped

1 small hot chilli, deseeded and finely
   chopped

2 garlic cloves, crushed

1 tablespoon tomato purée

1 tablespoon ground coriander

1/2 teaspoon cayenne pepper

100g (4oz) feta cheese, crumbled

sauces and spice mixes

✳ Hot lime and chilli pickle

This fiery pickle is a staple of Indian cooking. Serve as a dip, with poppadoms, or as an accompaniment to main courses. It is also good mixed with yoghurt and used as a dip for kebabs or vegetables. The flavour is quite tart, so if you prefer a sweeter pickle, add 2 tablespoons of honey

Makes about 225–300g (8–10 oz)

6 limes

4 tablespoons sea salt

300ml (1/2 pint) fresh lemon juice

6 garlic cloves, crushed

4 green chillies, thinly sliced

3 tablespoons ground cumin

2 tablespoons My curry paste
(see p154) or curry powder

100ml (3 1/2 fl oz) sesame oil

Wash the limes, place them in a saucepan with half the salt and pour in enough water to cover – about 600ml (1 pint). Bring to the boil, then remove from the heat and leave to soak for 15 minutes or until the skins are soft. Drain the limes, dry them well and leave to cool.

Cut the limes into large pieces, removing the pips, then sprinkle over the rest of the salt and mix with all the remaining ingredients. Place in a sterilised jar, seal and keep for up to 1 week before using. Once opened, the pickle will keep for about a month in the refrigerator.

HOT TIP As a short cut, you could buy lime pickle from an Asian food shop and spike it with chilli.

Peppercorn mustard and anchovy mayonnaise

This tangy mayonnaise is good with grilled or deep-fried fish and with fish cakes.

Pound the anchovy fillets in a mortar or crush them with a fork in a bowl. Add the egg yolks, vinegar and mustard and mix together. Gradually whisk in the olive oil, drop by drop at first, to form an emulsion.

Season to taste with salt and pepper.

Makes about 200ml (7fl oz)

2 anchovy fillets, rinsed and dried

2 egg yolks

2 tablespoons white wine vinegar

1 tablespoon green peppercorn mustard

150ml (1/4 pint) olive oil

Salt and freshly ground black pepper

Green peppercorn béarnaise sauce

Place the vinegar, bay leaf, peppercorns and tarragon stalks in a small saucepan, simmer until the vinegar is reduced by half and then strain.

Place egg yolks and the vinegar reduction in a bowl set over a pan of simmering water, making sure the water does not touch the base of the bowl. Whisk the mixture until it is thick enough to leave a ribbon on the surface when trailed from the whisk. Add the clarified butter a little at a time, whisking continually, until the sauce forms an emulsion. Stir in the lemon juice, season with salt and the cayenne pepper and fold in the green peppercorn purée. The sauce can be kept warm for up to 2 hours before use as long as it is at the right temperature – I find a vacuum flask ideal for the purpose.

HOT TIP To clarify butter, heat it gently in a small pan until it begins to boil. Boil for 2 minutes, then pour off the clarified butter though a fine conical strainer or a muslin-lined sieve, leaving the white, milky sediment in the pan.

4 tablespoons white wine vinegar

1 small bay leaf

1 teaspoon black peppercorns, lightly cracked (see Hot Tip on p28)

A few tarragon stalks

2 egg yolks

225g (8oz) unsalted butter, clarified (see Hot Tip)

1 tablespoon lemon juice

A pinch of cayenne pepper

50g (2oz) tin of green peppercorns, drained, rinsed and puréed

Salt

VARIATIONS

Smoky pepper béarnaise Replace the green peppercorns and cayenne with 1 large red pepper, roasted, peeled and puréed, and 1 teaspoon of smoked paprika.

Chilli béarnaise Replace the green peppercorns and cayenne with 1 tablespoon of hot chilli sauce.

Mustard béarnaise Replace the green peppercorns and cayenne with 1 tablespoon of wholegrain mustard.

Horseradish béarnaise Replace the green peppercorns and cayenne with 1 tablespoon of grated horseradish.

Hot achiote baste

Achiote seeds come from the annatto tree and are popular in the Yucatan peninsula of Mexico. They have a brick-red colour and an earthy flavour. Ready-made achiote paste is available but if you are using seeds you will need to soak them in water overnight and then grind them to a paste. Achiote baste can be brushed on to meat and left to marinate for 1 hour before grilling, then used to baste the meat during cooking.

Place the chillies in a blender with all the dry ingredients and blitz to a paste, adding the liquids a little at a time to form a purée.

Makes about 175ml (6fl oz)

3 ancho chillies, roasted (see p8) and thinly sliced

2 garlic cloves, crushed

1/2 teaspoon ground allspice

1 teaspoon cumin seeds, toasted in a dry frying pan

1 tablespoon achiote paste (or 11/2 teaspoons achiote seeds)

1 tablespoon olive oil

2 tablespoons white wine vinegar

6 tablespoons fresh orange juice

* Mexican chilli sauce

Serve this classic Mexican sauce with rolled tortillas or stir it into rice dishes and soups.

Put the roasted ancho and guajillo chillies in a pan, pour over enough boiling water to cover them and simmer for 5 minutes. Remove from the heat and leave to soak for about 30 minutes, until soft. Drain the chillies, reserving the soaking liquid, and put them in a blender with half the liquid. Add the chicken stock or water, garlic, cumin seeds and cloves and blend until smooth. Season with salt, then finish with the lime juice. Store in the fridge, where it will keep for 1 week.

Makes about 450ml (3/4 pint)

4 ancho chillies, roasted (see p8)

4 guajillo chillies, roasted (see p8)

200ml (7fl oz) chicken stock or water

4 garlic cloves, chopped

1/4 teaspoon cumin seeds

2 cloves

Juice of 1 lime

Salt

Horseradish sauce

This is very easy to make and so much better than commercial horseradish sauce. Besides having it with your Sunday roast, you could try it with Italian charcuterie or smoked fish such as trout, mackerel and eel. It also makes a good topping for beetroot soup, mixed with a little yoghurt.

Lightly whip the double cream until it begins to thicken enough to hang from the whisk without dropping. Gently fold in the crème fraîche, horseradish, wine vinegar and mustard, then season to taste. Add the chives, if using. Refrigerate until ready to serve.

Makes about 300ml (1/2 pint)

6 tablespoons double cream

4 tablespoons crème fraîche

3 tablespoons grated horseradish root

1 tablespoon white wine vinegar

1 teaspoon Dijon mustard

2 tablespoons chopped chives (optional)

Salt and freshly ground black pepper

* The classic American cocktail sauce
(hot tomato and horseradish)

This is nothing like the British cocktail sauce. It has a terrific flavour and really livens up seafood such as lobster and prawns. It also makes a good dip for vegetables.

Mix all of the ingredients together in a bowl, adding salt and pepper to taste. The sauce can be kept in the fridge for about a week but will lose its freshness after a couple of days.

Makes 300ml (1/2 pint)

300ml (1/2 pint) tomato ketchup

2 tablespoons grated horseradish root

1 garlic clove, crushed

3 tablespoons lemon juice

3 drops of Tabasco sauce

Salt and freshly ground black pepper

Asian sweet chilli sauce

Place all the ingredients in a food processor and blend until the texture is fine. Store in the fridge. It will keep for up to 1 month, or longer if you bottle it in a sterilised jar.

Makes about 300ml (1/2 pint)

1kg (2 1/4 lb) red serrano chillies, stems removed

5cm (2in) piece of fresh root ginger, chopped

2 garlic cloves, crushed

2 teaspoons rice wine vinegar

1 tablespoon caster sugar

2 teaspoons lime juice

Chilli jelly

This makes an excellent accompaniment to cold meats. I also like it brushed over chicken during roasting for a wonderfully hot, sweet and sticky glaze.

Gently heat the redcurrant jelly in a pan until dissolved. In a blender, blitz together all the remaining ingredients and then add to the jelly. Bring to the boil, reduce the heat and cook for about 30 minutes, until the jelly is thick and syrupy. Transfer to a bowl and leave to cool. **This** may be kept in a covered container for up to one month in the fridge.

250g (9oz) redcurrant jelly
1 habanero chilli, deseeded and chopped
1 red pepper, chopped
Juice of 1 lemon
2 drops of Tabasco sauce
2 tablespoons cider vinegar

Chilli and raisin jam

Depending on the strength of the chillies you use, this varies from hot to extremely hot! Serve as a dip for oriental-style dishes such as spring rolls or tempura. It also makes an excellent burger relish and can be cooked with vegetables, like the Sweet and sour baby onions on page 92.

Put the vinegar and sugar in a small pan and bring to the boil. Add the raisins and cook to a light caramel; the liquid should be syrupy. Stir in the shallots, chillies, ginger, garlic and fish sauce, then remove from the heat and leave to cool slightly. Place in a blender and blitz to a coarse purée.

Makes about 600ml (1 pint)
200ml (7fl oz) rice vinegar
125g (4½oz) soft brown sugar
150g (5oz) raisins
4 shallots, finely chopped
450g (1lb) red serrano chillies, deseeded and chopped
1 tablespoon finely chopped fresh root ginger
2 garlic cloves, crushed
1 teaspoon nam pla (Thai fish sauce)

* Chilli sambal

This makes a great dip for deep-fried fish and meat. It is also good added to stir-fries to enliven the flavours.

Deseed and slice the chillies. Gently heat the oil in a frying pan, add the shallots and garlic and cook until softened. Add the chillies and cook for 5 minutes, then stir in the tomatoes, sugar, nam pla and 100ml (3½fl oz) of water. Cook over a moderate heat for 10 minutes, then stir in the lime juice. Purée in a blender and season to taste with salt. Leave to cool, then store in the refrigerator in a sealed container. It will keep for up to a week, longer if bottled in a sterilised jar.

HOT TIP To sterilise jars, wash them thoroughly in hot soapy water, then rinse well and place on a baking tray. Dry in an oven preheated to 140°C/275°F/gas mark 1.

Makes about 300ml (1/2 pint)
8 large red Thai chillies
2 tablespoons vegetable oil
5 shallots, thinly sliced
4 garlic cloves, sliced
2 tomatoes, skinned, cut into wedges and deseeded
1 tablespoon brown sugar
1 teaspoon nam pla (Thai fish sauce)
2 teaspoons lime juice
Salt

CHILLI JELLY

Jalapeño and green tomato salsa

This is a good all-purpose salsa. Try it with grilled fish or seafood, kebabs, or classic Mexican dishes such as tacos and fajitas.

Combine all the ingredients in a bowl, adding salt and pepper to taste.

Leave to marinate for 1 hour before use to allow the flavours to meld.

450g (1lb) green tomatoes, deseeded and chopped

4 spring onions, finely shredded

6 tablespoons chopped coriander

2 jalapeño chillies, deseeded and chopped

1 garlic clove, crushed

Juice of 2 limes

2 tablespoons maple syrup

Salt and freshly ground black pepper

Hot Mexican salsa

Gently heat the oil in a pan, add the garlic, onion and chillies, then remove from the heat and leave to cool.

Stir in all the remaining ingredients. Leave to marinate for at least 2 hours before use to allow the flavours to meld.

2 tablespoons vegetable oil

3 garlic cloves, crushed

1 onion, finely chopped

1 habanero chilli, deseeded and finely chopped

2 jalapeño chillies, deseeded and finely chopped

450g (1lb) plum tomatoes, cut into 1cm (1/2in) dice

Juice of 2 limes

1/2 teaspoon dried oregano or 1 tablespoon fresh oregano

2 tablespoons maple syrup or honey

A pinch each of ground cumin and salt

4 tablespoons chopped coriander

Caribbean mojo

The habanero chilli gives this fruity salsa a powerful bite. Serve with grilled fish or meat. I particularly like it with tuna burgers or grilled lobster.

Place the diced mango, pineapple and avocado in a bowl, then mix in the lime and orange juice, coriander, sugar, chilli and spring onions.

Season with salt and feshly ground black pepper. Cover and leave to stand for about 30 minutes before use.

1 mango, peeled, stoned and cut into 5mm (1/4in) dice

50g (2oz) pineapple, cut into 5mm (1/4in) dice

1 avocado, peeled, stoned and cut into 5mm (1/4in) dice

Juice of 2 limes

75ml (21/2fl oz) orange juice

2 tablespoons chopped coriander

A pinch of sugar

1 habanero chilli, deseeded and finely diced

4 spring onions, shredded

Salt and freshly ground black pepper

✳ Aromatic chilli oil

Makes about 600ml (1 pint)

4 jalapeño or serrano chillies
600ml (1 pint) vegetable or groundnut oil

Chilli oil can be stored indefinitely in a cool, dry place, away from direct sunlight. However, I prefer to use it within four months, otherwise the flavour begins to lose its freshness. It is wonderful in all manner of dishes, such as dressings, soups and salads, and to spice up sauces and stir-fries. Below is my simple recipe for chilli oil, together with a few variations on the theme from around the world.

Cut the chillies in half to expose the seeds (if you prefer a milder oil, leave the chillies whole). Gently heat the oil in a pan, then add the chillies. Leave over a moderate heat for about 5–10 minutes, then remove from the heat and allow to infuse overnight in the pan.

The next day, remove the chillies from the oil, strain the oil into sterilised bottles and seal.

HOT TIP If, like me, you prefer the oil to have a real kick, leave the chillies in it when bottling.

VARIATIONS

South American chilli oil Replace the chillies with 1 shredded habanero chilli. Add 1 tablespoon of fresh oregano, 1/2 teaspoon of allspice, 2 garlic cloves, peeled, and 1 bay leaf.

Indian chilli oil Add 1 tablespoon each of roasted cumin seeds, fenugreek, black mustard seeds and crushed cardamom seeds.

Oriental chilli oil Add 11/2 teaspoons of toasted Szechuan peppercorns, 2 star anise and 4 tablespoons of sesame oil.

Smoky guacamole en molcajete with chilli oil

Molcajete is the Mexican name for a mortar and pestle, which is used to make the guacamole. Serve as a dip for crudités, rolled up in tortillas, or as an accompaniment to poached salmon.

Put the roasted chipotle chilli in a bowl, cover with hot water and leave to soak for 30 minutes. Drain and chop finely.

Cut the avocado in half, remove the stone and peel off the skin. Cut each half in half again. Heat a ridged grill pan (or, better still, a barbecue grill), brush the avocado wedges with the olive oil and grill on both sides until they are lightly browned but not heated through; do not let them brown too much or they will be bitter. Leave to cool.

Crush the garlic in a mortar and pestle, pressing on it to release as much juice as possible. Add the avocado and crush with the garlic. Then add the chopped chipotle chilli, onion and coriander. Finally mix in the lime juice and the pomegranate seeds, if using, then season with salt and pepper. Transfer to a serving dish, pour the chilli oil on top and serve.

1/2 chipotle chilli, roasted (see p8)

1 firm but ripe avocado

1 tablespoon olive oil

1 garlic clove, peeled

1 onion, finely chopped

1 tablespoon chopped coriander

Juice of 1 lime

Seeds from 1 pomegranate (optional)

2 tablespoons South American chilli oil (see p152)

Salt and freshly ground black pepper

My curry paste

Heat a large frying pan over a high heat. When hot, add all the whole spices and toast, shaking the pan frequently, until they begin to give off a rich aroma. Remove from the pan and leave to cool.

Grind the toasted spices in a spice mill or coffee grinder – or in a pestle and mortar – and mix in the ginger, turmeric and cognac. Place in a bowl and stir in the oil to form a thick paste. This should keep for about a month in the fridge, although I always find I use it up pretty quickly.

2 tablespoons coriander seeds

2 tablespoons fennel seeds

1 tablespoon cardamom pods

1 tablespoon black peppercorns

2 teaspoons cumin seeds

1 teaspoon fenugreek seeds

1 teaspoon black mustard seeds

1 cinnamon stick

5 cloves

1 teaspoon ground ginger

1 tablespoon ground turmeric

2 teaspoons cayenne pepper

About 2 tablespoons vegetable oil

* Ethiopian berbere

Place the roasted chillies in a bowl, pour over 300ml (1/2 pint) of boiling water and leave to soak for 30 minutes. Meanwhile, heat a heavy-based frying pan, add the peppercorns and cumin seeds and toss them over a moderate heat until they become fragrant.

Drain the chillies, reserving the soaking liquid, and place them in a blender. Add the grated onion, garlic and ground spices as well as the toasted peppercorns and cumin seeds. Add a little of the chilli soaking liquid and blitz to a smooth paste, then add the oil and blitz again.

Place the mixture in a small pan and cook over a low heat for 10 minutes, stirring frequently so it doesn't burn. Remove from the heat and put aside to cool. Transfer the berbere to an airtight container, seal well and store in the refrigerator for up to 2 weeks.

HOT TIP If you want a slightly milder sauce, remove the seeds from the chillies.

Makes about 150ml (1/4 pint)

25g (1oz) dried red chillies, such as ancho or De Arbol, roasted (see p8)

1 teaspoon black peppercorns

2 teaspoons cumin seeds

1 onion, grated

2 garlic cloves, crushed

1 teaspoon ground cardamom

1/4 teaspoon ground allspice

1/4 teaspoon ground cinnamon

1/2 teaspoon ground coriander

1/2 teaspoon ground ginger

2 tablespoons smoked paprika

3 tablespoons groundnut oil

Green Thai curry paste

Heat a heavy-based frying pan over a low heat, add the coriander seeds, cumin seeds and aniseed and toast for 2 minutes, until they give off their aroma. Transfer to a spice mill or coffee grinder and blitz to a fine powder.

Put all the rest of the ingredients except the shrimp paste in a blender and blitz. Add the ground spices and shrimp paste and blitz again to a smooth paste. Store in an airtight container in the fridge, where it should keep for about a month.

VARIATION

Red Thai curry paste Prepare as above but substitute 6 red serrano or jalapeno chillies for the green chillies, increase the garlic to 8 cloves and use 12 black peppercorns instead of 1/8 teaspoon. Add 3 tablespoons of vegetable oil with the shrimp paste.

Makes about 250ml (8fl oz)

1 tablespoon coriander seeds

1 teaspoon cumin seeds

1 teaspoon whole aniseed

12 green bird's eye or Thai chillies, chopped

2 shallots, chopped

3 garlic cloves, crushed

2.5cm (1in) piece of fresh galangal, peeled and chopped

2 lemongrass sticks, outer layers removed, chopped

8 kaffir lime leaves

1 tablespoon coriander, stalks and roots only

1/2 teaspoon black peppercorns

2 teaspoons blachan *(dried shrimp paste)*

* Harissa

Heat the oil in a large, heavy-based pan. Add all the ingredients except the salt and pepper and cook over a medium heat for about 5 minutes or until the red pepper has softened. Add 300ml (1/2 pint) of water and bring to the boil. Reduce the heat and simmer gently for 10 minutes or until the pepper is really soft. Purée in a blender until smooth. Season to taste with salt and pepper and leave to cool. This will keep in the fridge for 10 days or in the freezer for 1 month.

1 tablespoon vegetable oil

1 large red pepper, finely chopped

3 red chillies, deseeded and chopped

2 garlic cloves, crushed

1 tablespoon ground coriander

1 tablespoon ground cumin

1 tablespoon ground caraway

2 tablespoons tomato purée

Salt and freshly ground black pepper

Asian blackened spice mix

This is an adaptation of the classic Creole-Cajun spice mix – an idea I had one day when I wanted to prepare a spicy Asian-style fish dish. Flavoured with cardamom and fennel seeds, it is great with meat as well as fish.

Heat a heavy-based frying pan over a high heat, then add the whole spices and toast them, shaking the pan frequently, until they begin to give off a rich aroma. Place the toasted spices in a spice mill or coffee grinder, add the turmeric, cayenne and ginger and blitz to a powder. (If you have time on your hands you could pound them in a pestle and mortar instead.) Store in an airtight container.

2 tablespoons coriander seeds

2 tablespoons fennel seeds

1 tablespoon cardamom pods

1 tablespoon black peppercorns

2 teaspoons cumin seeds

1 teaspoon fenugreek seeds

1 teaspoon black mustard seeds

5 cloves

1 cinnamon stick

1 tablespoon ground turmeric

2 teaspoons cayenne pepper

1 teaspoon ground ginger

Colombo spice mix

This Sri Lankan curry powder is made with roasted basmati rice, which may sound unusual but gives it a wonderful nutty flavour.

Heat a heavy-based frying pan over a medium heat, add the rice and toast for 3–4 minutes, until golden. Transfer to a bowl. Put the whole spices in the pan for 3–4 minutes, shaking the pan frequently, until lightly toasted and fragrant. Add the spices to the rice and leave to cool. Blitz the mixture to a fine powder in a spice mill or coffee grinder, then add the turmeric. Store in an airtight container.

8 tablespoons basmati rice

6 tablespoons cumin seeds

8 tablespoons coriander seeds

2 tablespoons black mustard seeds

2 tablespoons black peppercorns

2 tablespoons fenugreek seeds

2 teaspoons whole cloves

8 tablespoons ground turmeric

Blackened Cajun spice mix

A punchy spice mix that originates from Louisiana and is used extensively in Cajun and Creole cooking. It is very adaptable and can be added to all sorts of fish and meat dishes.

Place all the ingredients in a spice mill or coffee grinder and blitz to a fine powder. Transfer the spice mix to an airtight container and seal well before storing.

1 tablespoon salt

1 tablespoon hot paprika

1 teaspoon garlic powder

1 teaspoon black peppercorns

1 teaspoon chilli powder (or cayenne pepper)

1 tablespoon dried thyme

1 tablespoon dried oregano

2 teaspoons ground cumin

Sri Lankan spice mix

The coriander, cumin, fennel seeds and fenugreek need to be dry-roasted separately, as they tend to darken at different stages: heat a small, heavy-based frying pan, add each spice and, shaking the pan frequently, roast until the seeds darken slightly and begin to give off their aroma. Transfer to a plate and set aside.

Put all the remaining ingredients in the pan and dry-roast for about 30 seconds, until they give off a rich aroma. Place all the ingredients in a spice mill or coffee grinder and blitz to a fine powder. Store in an airtight container.

6 tablespoons coriander seeds

3 tablespoons cumin seeds

1 tablespoon fennel seeds

1 teaspoon fenugreek seeds

2 teaspoons chilli powder

2 teaspoons ground cinnamon

1 teaspoon cloves

5 dried curry leaves

10 cardamom pods

Barbecue spice mix

This adaptable spice mix can be sprinkled over vegetables or rubbed on fish or meat before barbecuing or grilling. Like all spice mixes, it keeps well in an airtight container for about a month but the flavour will gradually deteriorate if it is stored much longer than this.

Put all of the ingredients in a bowl and mix until thoroughly combined. Transfer to an airtight container and seal well before storing.

4 tablespoons dried red chilli flakes

3 tablespoons paprika

1 tablespoon ground cumin

1 tablespoon ground coriander

1 tablespoon caster sugar

2 teaspoons salt

1 teaspoon mustard powder

1 teaspoon freshly ground black pepper

1 teaspoon dried thyme

1 teaspoon mild curry powder

2 teaspoons cayenne pepper

Index

Acknowledgements

During the writing of this book, there have been many people whose help, encouragement and enthusiasm has been invaluable.

My very grateful thanks go to:

Linda Tubby for preparing and styling the food shots for photography and for making the dishes look delicious.

Jane Middleton for her usual superb editing of my recipes. She is simply 'The Best'.

Gus Filgate, friend and truly exceptional photographer.

Róisín Nield for sourcing such wonderful props.

Vanessa Courtier for her beautiful design.

Fiona Lindsay and Linda Shanks, my agents for just about everything.

Lara King for her endless hours typing the manuscript.

Michael and Joy Michaud for their help, friendship and for providing some truly wonderful fresh chillies for photography. (Peppers by Post: Sea Spring Farm, West Bexington, Dorchester, Dorset, Tel: 01308 897892).

The Cool Chilli Company for providing some fantastic dried and powdered chilli varieties (PO Box 5702, London W11 2ES, Tel: 0207 229 9360).

Geoffrey Gelardi, Managing Director and my dedicated kitchen brigade, especially Justin Woods, Christophe Poupardin and Samantha Mills for helping with photographic preparations, especially during busy times.

Finally a huge thank you to Kyle Cathie, and her dedicated team, especially Sheila Boniface for all the hard work support and friendship and for believing that this book might be a 'hot' idea to publish.